Our Bodies Are Alive

Our Bodies Are Alive

Self-Literacy as an Embodied Healing
and Liberative Practice

Bridget L. Piggue

CASCADE *Books* · Eugene, Oregon

OUR BODIES ARE ALIVE
Self-Literacy as an Embodied Healing and Liberative Practice

Copyright © 2025 Bridget L. Piggue. All rights reserved. Except for brief quotations in critical publications or reviews, no part of this book may be reproduced in any manner without prior written permission from the publisher. Write: Permissions, Wipf and Stock Publishers, 199 W. 8th Ave., Suite 3, Eugene, OR 97401.

Cascade Books
An Imprint of Wipf and Stock Publishers
199 W. 8th Ave., Suite 3
Eugene, OR 97401

www.wipfandstock.com

PAPERBACK ISBN: 978-1-6667-6602-8
HARDCOVER ISBN: 978-1-6667-6603-5
EBOOK ISBN: 978-1-6667-6604-2

Cataloguing-in-Publication data:

Names: Piggue, Bridget L., author.

Title: Our bodies are alive : self-literacy as an embodied healing and liberative practice / Bridget L. Piggue.

Description: Eugene, OR : Cascade Books, 2025 | Includes bibliographical references.

Identifiers: ISBN 978-1-6667-6602-8 (paperback) | ISBN 978-1-6667-6603-5 (hardcover) | ISBN 978-1-6667-6604-2 (ebook)

Subjects: LCSH: Womanist theology. | Black theology. | Feminist theology. | Theology, Practical.

Classification: BT83.9 .P55 2025 (paperback) | BT83.9 .P55 (ebook)

VERSION NUMBER 04/28/25

I dedicate this work to an amazing woman, my mother, Jessie Lankford. Her unwavering love, deep commitment, and assiduous sacrifice on behalf of those she loved paved the way for opportunities she could only imagine for herself. It is because she loved so hard and so fiercely that I am able to stand resilient and strong; a woman armed with hope and the resources to carry forward the message of healing through loving fiercely. As she looks upon this accomplishment, I know beyond a shadow of doubt that she is "So Very, Very Proud of Me!"

I also dedicate this work to Christine Perkins, my grandmother, who kept me close during the early years of my life. Though we met for only a short time before she left this realm of existence, I feel that I have known her intimately. Thank you, Madea, for the free spirit that resides within me. I am told it is a lot like yours. To Aunt Jessie, who managed to simply enjoy life despite limitations placed on women of her time, and to Aunt Carrie, who managed to live long and strong, I honor you. To Aunt Jack, Nell, Joyce, Gloria, Bren, and Pam, each of you affirmed that I was somebody, that I was special, and that I belonged. I stand on your shoulders in deep gratitude along with Aunt Deb, who continues to carry the torch for us. And to my other mothers, Lula Perkins, Lula Todd (Tott), and my paternal grandmother, who wanted very much to know me, I honor your legacy along with those I do not know but whose blood runs through my veins. I live in hope that you are pleased with this accomplishment and that a dream has been realized through me. *Ashe*!

Contents

Acknowledgments | ix

Introduction | xiii

1 Bodies Under Duress: A Womanist's Dilemma | 1
2 Toward an Understanding of Body-Mind Connection | 10
3 A Necessary Path: Unearthing Our Body Narratives | 16
4 African American Clergy Women Narrating Their Sacred Stories | 26
5 Healing Approaches | 66
6 What Select Neuroscientific Perspectives and Somatic Psychology Offer a Conversation on Healing Practice | 78
7 FIERCELY Model | 95
8 A Womanist Theological Reflection: The Cannanite Woman Archetype (Matthew 15:21–28) | 105

Appendix: African American Clergy Women Interview Responses | 115
Bibliography | 145

Acknowledgments

I WOULD LIKE TO thank the ten women who graciously welcomed me into the sacred spaces of their hearts and minds, offering voice to this study. They are resilient, powerful women to whom I owe a deep debt of gratitude. May you continue to love yourselves fiercely!

To the committee members that helped me birth this work, thank you for your commitment and support over the years. It has been invaluable. I am especially grateful to Dr. Emmanuel Lartey for perceiving in me what I many times could not perceive within myself. You held my tears with care when times were rough and held me equally accountable to my best work. Your academic integrity and brilliant scholarship, buoyed by a deep and abiding spiritual force, provided the type of energy any person would desire along a scholarly journey. I offer my sincere appreciation, love, and respect. To Dr. Carolyn McCrary, you have been a model of Womanism, offering wisdom, nurture, care, practical scholarship, and authentic sisterhood that has been sustaining beyond words. To Dr. Edward Wimberly, you have been "clutch" at very crucial points along my journey. Thank you for showing up with academic excellence, clarity, and unmatched scholarship. You have been a rock for me at times when I needed you most. I honor you and Dr. Anne Wimberly for your investment in me. To Dr. Karen Scheib, thank you for helping me to understand that scholars are diverse and that the practitioner's voice has a profound place at the table.

To my greatest supporter and fan, David Elijah Piggue, who has shared his mother with many over the years, thank you for understanding my quest for academic excellence and purposeful living. You never doubted my love or your priority in my life. Thank you dear heart, I am grateful to

Acknowledgments

call you son. To my sister Nesie, the other ordained clergy woman in the family, you have always been there for me, ready with feedback and the honest critique I needed. You, along with Rhonda, my best girlfriend, and Diedra, Deval, Janet, Samantha, Shirley, Claire, Susan, Donna, Nina, Paul, Lisa, Candace, Bridgette, and Dee, you all made me feel so smart and gifted. The love you have given is simply unmatched! Isom, my brother, your quiet and loving support runs deep and has always been appreciated. To the rest of the Lankford's, my aunties and uncles, nieces and nephews, cousins and other family near and far, I say thank you for the prayers and hope sent my way. Mike B, thank you for being there for me, partnering, supporting, caring, and artistically capturing beautiful and significant moments along this sometimes arduous path. To my Atonement church family, good girlfriends, other friends, and dance community, I am grateful for worship, outings, events, and dances that helped to bridge the gap when I needed breaks, inspiration, and praise—all of it mattered in the entire scheme of things. And to my doctoral dialogue partner, colleague, and friend, Dr. Melva Sampson, you were a stabilizing force, honest shooter, and just good company while meeting the challenges of all that came along with our trek. Love you! To Dr. Gregory Ellison, as you took me seriously, offered wisdom, excellence, brilliance, and friendship, I am proud to call you brother and friend. I truly have nothing but love for you. To my friend and sister elder Joy Ponder Bates, you have been wind beneath my wings, urging me "not to take too long because the world was waiting on what this work offers." I felt strengthened by you in every step. Rest in power, my sister. I miss you on this side.

To my Emory Midtown family, I could not have asked for a better staff of leaders. You allow me to exhale and to know all will be well. Cynthia, Jose, Byron, Joshua, Erica, Hannah, Brenda Cecile, Belinda, Galetha, Joe, Jordan, Francisco, and Sara, whose excellence and detailed eye helped me cross the final leg of this book journey, you are God's very special people. To Emory Spiritual Health and the ACPE community, you are my colleagues, Clinical Pastoral Educators and Candidates, residents, interns, fellows, and professional chaplains in this very important work. I drew a great deal from what we do in order to complete this book. Thank you for listening to my ideas over the years, reflecting back to me in dialogue, and being models of how healing and transformation can take place. I want to especially thank Maureen Shelton, my sister who holds love for God's people in a way that is other worldly, and Joan Murray, whose dedication to pray for me daily

Acknowledgments

kept me lifted and strong. Robin, Stephen, Tim, CG, Va'Nechia, Darrel, Tamekia, Eloise, Cheryl, and Beth, thank you for always making me feel that my work was interesting and worth taking precious time to hear. To Eugene Robinson, my wise colleague and father figure, you've given me foundations in this field of pastoral/spiritual care that are more profound than you can ever know. You taught me how to be an integrated self, and for that I will forever be grateful. To my executive director Dr. George Grant, it has been a privilege and blessing to be able to complete this work while working for Emory Spiritual Health. I have never taken that for granted and in deep gratitude, I have welcomed your support. I most importantly want to thank you for introducing me to the word "Self-Literacy," as you see it has grounded and significantly informed my work.

To Dr. David and Dr. Claudette A. Copeland, my spiritual father and mother, you gave me an amazing foundation from which to launch in ministry. Thank you for loving and seeing me through some very good and tough times. The seeds you planted many years ago are bearing fruit. I can't thank God enough for your investment and guidance. And to my entire New Creation Christian Fellowship family, I have felt your love and support every step of the way.

To Dr. Mark Lomax and the First African Church community, thank you for allowing me to stretch my wings and explore indigenous spirituality as I never had before joining such a special community. Many of the insights I use in this work were nurtured at FAC through presentations by spiritual practitioners and exposure to holistic healing modalities. It was all so very powerful! *Ashe*!

To my colleagues and friends who pastor churches and are engaged in healing work on a daily basis, thank you for the wisdom, profound conversation, sermons, workshops, and enlightening healing experiences. Our time together helped to enhance my work of integrating theory and practice. You are appreciated.

I want to also thank the theologians, professors, and guides who stood ready to provide vision, a reference, or simply an encouraging word, having themselves walked this road before: Dr. Gregory Ellison, Dr. Noel Erskine, Dr. Teresa Fry-Brown, Dr. Lee Butler, Dr. Carol Watkins-Ali, Dr. Trina Armstrong, Dr. Stephanie Crumpton, Dr. Will Coleman, Dr. Nicole Phillips, Dr. Robert Franklin, Dr. Wynnetta Wimberly, Dr. Teresa Snorton, Dr. Christina Hicks, Dr. Jean Beedoe, Dr. Keith Slaughter, Dr. Maisha Handy, Dr. Rosetta Ross, Dr. Ron Bonner, Dr. Phillis Sheppard, Dr. David A.

Acknowledgments

Hooker, Dr. Catrice Glenn, Dr. Jacquelyn Grant, Dr. Willie Goodman, Dr. Bill Harkins, Dr. Christina Jones, Dr. Itihari Toure, Dr. Anthony Granberry, Dr. Beverly Wallace, and numerous others, to you I am grateful.

Introduction

"Our Bodies are Alive!" is a statement I have often used to open seminars on the topic of Self-Literacy.[1] On many occasions I was met with a blank stare as if to convey, "Of course it is, and . . .?" My next step was to repeat the statement for emphasis before sharing that statistically many people see themselves, as a self, from the top of their head to their chin, likely because it is a logical location for the brain.[2] The remainder of the body was relegated to what was seemingly an external object, something to be hauled or towed, and not quite regarded enough to be equally central in focus. I continued to share that our bodies appear to become a valued study subject or of greater interest when either sickness or wounding imposes, certain physical ailments began to limit routine function, or at another place on the body continuum, sexual awareness peaks. A potential exception to this delayed interest may lie with those born with a physical condition or disability that necessitated constant attention or engagement with the body early in life, thus heightening focused attention and levels of understanding the body that may be uncommon to many.

In this book my goal is an invitation to recognize that our Bodies are indeed alive, and because they are alive there is an inherent petition for consistent interfacing and communication. A respect for such dialogue within can inform transformation and serve as a foundation for building useful healing and liberative practices. This invitation includes recognizing

1. Self Literacy: The two words together "self and literacy" are my use of common terms compounded to describe the knowledge and competence one possesses about their "self" and the essential qualities distinguishing them from any other.
2. Starmans and Bloom, "What Do You Think You Are?"

Introduction

that for far too long there has been an underrepresented and underappreciated regard for the rich knowledge and deep wisdom our bodies hold. I suggest that the path forward is through critical reflection and intentional embrace of what I've referred to as Self-Literacy. Self-Literacy and growth in the area of self-relationship recognizes that our bodies are in communication with everything internal and external in proximity and that it is crucial for us to take charge of the narrative that is being created about us and engaged regardless of our perceived participation. We are the most important relationship we will ever have, and for numerous reasons, some of which will be explored in this book, this fact can escape us until we are literally forced to pay closer attention to her. Admittedly, this could sound a bit odd, especially if one does not view their body alive in this manner. If noted, I chose to use my personal pronoun "her" in third person, as if "she" were another. Building upon the invitation that has been issued, one might consider a particular lens through which to view themselves throughout the remainder of this book. I propose the utilization of personal pronouns as a means of humanizing your body and seeing "her" as another, but as another who is still you. I devised this practice while witnessing many who, without second thought, sacrifice themselves on behalf of another and quickly deny preference to their self-relationship. My rationale lied in the query, "If I could invite a person to view themselves as an external other, then perhaps they might engage in more care of *this* external other, who happens to be them." I called the practice "externalizing as a means to internalize the self." It was not intended as a mind trick, yet has proven to give persons a sense of grounding, presence and interaction with themselves in ways unexpected. I consequently felt it important to embrace and further develop this practice as normative because the health and well-being of numerous spiritual leaders were being negatively impacted as a result of similarly imposed self-sacrificial messages that I contend were etched within the canvas of their bodies. Curiosity was peaked enough to begin an even closer look at my own participation in self-sacrifice and corresponding, counter-productive behaviors in my life and health. Widening my lens even further, I also considered the reality of how it was affecting numerous women who belonged to or were closely aligned with my demographic. What I discovered is introduced in the chapters to follow and reveals not only concerns and challenges but also useful steps toward recovery, restoration, resilience, and hope.

1

Bodies Under Duress

A Womanist's Dilemma

THE LIVED EXPERIENCES OF many African American clergy women indicate that their bodies are under significant duress. They are among an alarming number of people who suffer pain physically, mentally, and spiritually due to historically unique challenges. Such challenges include embodied thought and internalized messages that reinforce a disparate sense of importance and value. However, as the conversation of value and justice transpires, those who have written and deliberated about the pain of African American clergy women's physical and mental suffering seem to limit spiritual, psychological, and theological discourse germane to the conversation. For instance, it appears that insufficient use is made of body intelligence and scientific factors that may offer additional insight and suggestions, particularly for addressing the care of her body, mind, and spirit while carrying the weight of pastoral ministry. I highlight the importance of self-literacy and self-relating in light of dialogue surrounding gender and body, the ways in which the body expresses somaticized conditions, and engaged responses that support the health and well-being of African American clergy women. Imaging, which also plays a crucial role in this type of healing work, not only serves as a function of intra-psychic developmental processes informed by social and cultural factors but also is foundational to one's identity formation in terms of spirituality, self-worth, and physical health. Often overlooked in the complex arguments surrounding gender, patriarchy, hierarchy, and humanity are the continued negative health outcomes that plague African American clergy women while deeply engaged in the fight against oppression on multiple levels.

African American clergy women have been commendably successful, often through the medium of womanist thought, in giving voice to their struggle against marginalization by oppressive structures and practices. The power of this voice has been revolutionary and empowering. It is a gift to be valued and protected as the health and continued well-being of African American clergy women hinges on its strength. However, in regard to the health and well-being of African American clergy women, there is reason for concern. This concern lies in the question of whether a clergy woman's health is compromised when residual pain from oppression she has previously experienced becomes the primary fuel for engaging very necessary arguments. Further complexity arises if self-awareness is nominal. Without significant conception of the impact of such residual pain, wherein embodied trauma and unhealed wounds are the source and impetus for leading passionate confrontation, then African American clergy women's health, along with the beauty and power of the liberative message of womanism, is jeopardized.

I in no way suggest overlooking the critical issues women face on an ongoing basis and have been sufficiently researched. On the contrary, it is my hope that the intellectually well-respected and courageous works of many womanist theologians and their advocates continue to illuminate and challenge despotic thinking. Such works include the critical analysis and suggested ways of deconstructing oppressive norms, as presented by Jacquelyn Grant in her trailblazing efforts to address the remnants in liberation and feminist theology's exclusion of the unique experiences that were and remain unequally translatable in the search for solutions related to the well-being of Black women.[1] Making use of diverse and relevant therapeutic approaches, Leslie Jackson and Beverly Green highlight disparities within the counseling context that have pathologized African American women when their experiences did not easily fit categories of clinical diagnostic manuals and resources. In their book *Psychotherapy with African American Women,* Jackson and Green confront these biases by bringing together the voices of seasoned clinicians and their reformulations of theory and technique that proved more beneficial in the face of stereotypes and myths, thus yielding more appropriate interventions with African American women.[2]

---

1. Grant, *White Women's Christ and Black Women's Jesus.*
2. Jackson and Greene, *Psychotherapy with African American Women,* xvi–xx.

Participating in liberating praxis, as clarified by Carroll Watkins Ali, has been a critical point of exploration through investigation of new strategies for the survival and liberation of African Americans. In addition, liberating praxis has been critical in helping to heal the Black psyche and transform American society. In true womanist form, Watkins Ali offers a practical model that begins with African American women's narrative as a way of exposing larger contextual issues related to survival and liberation. She reinforces the idea that a liberating praxis would have to focus on Blackness and freedom in order to encourage Black people to imagine God as Black like them and, as a result, shift in their self-esteem to feel empowered.[3] Similarly, Watkins Ali purports the need for Black women to imagine God as like them, thus benefitting from the same manner of shift in their self-esteem and feelings of empowerment. Re-authoring stories, as suggested by Edward Wimberly, supports and fosters greater mental health and clarity for the caregiver. Wimberly's important contribution offers a useful model for the personal work of pastoral caregivers and other clergy related to the practice of re-authoring myths from their narratives—"myths that have been potentially destructive of the growth and well-being of the self and others." Re-authoring then becomes a practice that "enables religious and professional caregivers to be more human and make use of their own healed inadequacies as sources of strength for ministry and caregiving."[4] It is my expectation that these and similar works will continue to play a significant role in the healing of African American clergy women's psychic pain, spiritual crisis, and physical bodies. My interest lies in reinforcing the importance of cries from the body, the messages she yields, and the necessity of her voice to be heard more clearly and considered equally profound within discussions about the health and well-being of African American clergy women.

Toward that end, bringing diverse disciplines together in dialogue helps to ground and generate respectful conversation and relevant ideas on the topic of the body. Important here is the suggestion that she, the body, houses core elements of each discipline and offers unique perspective through which to consider pertinent facets of African American clergy women's experiences. These disciplines include neuroscience, womanist theology, psychology, and indigenous spirituality.

---

3. Watkins Ali, *Survival and Liberation*, 38, 111.
4. Wimberly, *Recalling Our Own Stories*, xii.

A primary consideration in this integrative conversation is how certain neuroscientific perspectives, theological gleanings from womanist theology, and indigenous spirituality intersect and inform the creation of a useful pastoral psychological framework for constructive embodied thought and therapeutic healing approaches.

Sensitization to a number of factors ground such a framework and includes conceptions from bodies of knowledge in health science, body intelligence, social construction, religion, spirituality, ritual, and culture. Useful terminology found in the work of David Kruger, Stephanie Mitchem, and editors Roy Moodley and William West proved beneficial as resources for understanding core elements of this discourse.

Krueger offers an understanding of neuroscience as a field of study that focuses on the nervous system, including the brain, spinal cord, and network of sensory cells called neurons.[5] It is an interdisciplinary field that integrates several disciplines, including psychology, biology, chemistry, and physics. In the study of the nervous system, the field of neuroscience adds to a body of knowledge about human thought, emotion, and behavior. Particular to this topic is the focus on brain function with other systems of the body and how variations of body chemistry affect emotion and behavior. These ideas are consistent with an integrative view of the body and mind.

Mitchem's perspective on womanist theology is relevant and useful to any conversation about Black women but especially in relation to this topic. She asserts that womanist theology challenges all oppressive forces impeding Black woman's struggle for survival and for the development of a positive, productive, quality of life conducive to her, her family, and her communities' freedom and well-being.[6] I appreciate and invited a deeper understanding of this perspective as foundational to the healing and empowerment of African American clergy women as well as the creation of sound healing and liberative practices.

Moodley and West shed light on indigenous spirituality as the rich healing traditions of cultures from around the world used to work toward the empowerment, health, and healing of its people.[7]

As a member of African American clergy woman leaders who have been confronted with important decisions about personal and collective health, I was interested in the significantly large number within my

---

5. Krueger, *Integrating Body Self and Psychological Self*, xi.
6. Mitchem, *Introducing Womanist Theology*, 82.
7. Moodley and West, *Integrating Traditional Healing Practices*, xv.

demographic who face critical illnesses while offering ministry and care to others, and as mentioned previously, the underrepresented and underappreciated pieces of conversations on justice and liberation related to the intelligence that lies within our bodies. Critical scientific research offers useful insight and exploration of integrative health wherein the body and mind connections are taken seriously in the assessment of health outcomes. In an effort to make connections, through a resource entitled *The Body Has a Mind of Its Own*, I was introduced to the concept of "body mapping"— "the brain's ability to inform itself through the construction of maps formed when we interact with objects."[8] My curiosity piqued, and an immediate question loomed heavy about whether the experience of body mapping, as described above, impacts African American clergy women who engage the fight against oppression in a way that promotes the synthesis of energy to that of their oppressor?

In addition, I wondered if a synthesis of the oppressor's energy to theirs allowed their bodies to store inherent messages that may find expression in counter-productive ways? Antonio Demasio, the David Dornslife professor of Neuroscience, Psychology, and Neurology at the University of Southern California and author of *Self Comes to Mind: Constructing the Conscious Brain*, in a case wherein the oppressed and oppressor's energy share similarities, might assert that a person's neurotransmitters receive the energy source of a message and mimic it for storage within the brain and make it one's own point of reference for addressing the issue at hand, even in ways unintended.[9] Consequently, I question whether the same destructive energy has opportunity to form within the body and continuously release messages to the body unless intentional efforts are observed to prevent or decrease it? In this respect, I emphasize the importance and necessity for African American clergy women to craft healthy practices of

---

8. Read Blakeslee and Blakeslee, *Body Has a Mind of Its Own*, 7–12, where they expound upon body mantras, maps, and schemas. A definition of body mapping includes ideas taken from the noted pages and is explained as follows: "The brain's ability to inform itself through construction of maps formed when we interact with objects. Through this process the brain through mapping is creating images that serve as the mind's main currency. The construction of these maps never cease; they occur when we recall objects from the inside of our brain's memory, in our sleep, from objects that sit outside of us, from actions that occur around us, and all the relationships that objects and actions assume in time and space, relative to each other and to the organism of the body. All that sits outside the brain can be mimicked inside the brain's networks."

9. Damasio, *Self Comes to Mind*, 41–42, 68–69. For Demasio, brain and body are often used interchangeably.

speaking truth to power on their terms—not in a reactionary posture but in response by use of embodied power that may look very different than that to which she may have been accustomed.

Joy DeGruy Leary, a clinical psychologist, social worker, and former assistant professor at Portland State University, also offers critical examination of the influence embedded messages have on the current state of African descent persons, especially the implications they have for the body. DeGruy Leary, in her book *Post-Traumatic Slave Syndrome: America's Legacy of Enduring Injury and Healing*, asserts that "Post-Traumatic Slave Syndrome (PTSS)"[10] continues to have a profound impact on the lives of Black people decades after the formalized oppression of slavery. In this text, she emphasizes how the atrocity of the Maafa that occurred for decades still continues and persists in our bodies today.[11] DeGruy Leary goes on to say that, similar to PTSD, PTSS has symptoms that linger, having lasting effects that trigger a person's reaction to embedded messages, images, sounds, sights, and smells. Also similar to the concept of multi-generational transmission within Murray Bowen's Family Systems Theory, DeGruy Leary asserts that, for Black people, systemic racism and oppression result in multigenerational adaptive behaviors, some of which are positive, but others detrimental and destructive. She states that induced and learned stress-related issues continue to pass through generations, reinforcing the idea of familiarity that finds a way to present itself through embodied energy

---

10. See Leary, *Post Traumatic Slave Syndrome*, 13–14, where she defines "Post Traumatic Slave Syndrome" drawn from an understanding of "Post Traumatic Stress Disorder" and a definition of trauma. Trauma is as an injury caused by an outside, usually violent, force, event or experience. It is an injury that can be physical, emotional, psychological, and/or spiritual, upsetting equilibrium and a sense of well-being. If it is severe enough it can distort one's attitudes and beliefs, often resulting in dysfunctional behaviors which can produce unwanted consequences. She notes that these patterns can be magnified exponentially when a person repeatedly experiences severe trauma and can be made much worse when the traumas are caused by human beings. More poignantly applied to "Post Traumatic Slave Syndrome." this type of trauma identifies the slave experience as such and one of continual, violent attacks on the slave's body, mind, and spirit. Because slave men, women, and children were traumatized throughout their lives and the violent attacks persisted long after emancipation they adapted attitudes and behaviors to simply survive and those adaptations continue to manifest today in various ways.

11. Leary, *Post Traumatic Slave Syndrome*, 73. DeGruy Leary defines Maafa as the African Holocaust referring to the 1,500 years of suffering by Black Africans and the African Diaspora through slavery, colonialism, dehumanization, and exploitation. Important to note is that residual effects of this persecution continue to manifest in contemporary society.

that has been imposed through certain types of communication we receive, whether intentional or not.[12]

Dr. Christiane Northrup, MD, an OB-GYN physician specializing in women's holistic health, offers important information about similar dynamics and their impact on women, suggesting that the way in which a female thinks about her body has direct impact on how she relates to her body. In her book *Women's Bodies, Women's Wisdom: Creating Physical and Emotional Health and Healing,* Northrup writes:

> A thought held long enough and repeated enough becomes a belief. The belief then becomes biology. Beliefs are energetic forces that create the physical basis for our individual lives and our health. If we don't work through our emotional distress, we set ourselves up for physical distress because of biochemical effects that suppressed emotions have on our immune and endocrine systems. At any given time, our state of health reflects the sum total of our beliefs since birth.[13]

The idea of the mind-body connection and its intrinsic value in exploring health outcomes is significant as suggested in the quotation above. Important in Northrup's work is an understanding that the nature of energy exchange between the mind and body distinctly informs how we, as "matter," actually take shape and function. Northrup submits that "because matter includes the human cell, then cells are subject to take cues from the energy one generates as well as the energy of others around them, some of whom they may not even be in direct contact."[14]

Though interesting, facets of these ideas are hardly novel. Psychotherapy has long met the needs of addressing historical messages that manifest in emotional states and impact one's current function. My interest lies in enhancing the pastoral theological and spiritual health fields through incorporating these critical aspects of neuroscience into an integrative study of mind, body, and spirit while also yielding a pastoral psychological framework for constructive embodied thought and therapeutic healing approaches.

For African American clergy women, disembodied thought—*separated from or existing without the body*[15]—may be considered a betrayal of

12. Leary, *Post Traumatic Slave Syndrome*, 15–16.
13. Northrup, *Women's Bodies, Women's Wisdom*, 29.
14. Northrup, *Women's Bodies, Women's Wisdom*, 27.
15. Stevenson, "Disembodied," 501.

sorts that neglects the uniqueness and power of the female body housed in the persons of clergy women who carry the burden of a call to lead others. When perspectives and behaviors toward the female body do not consider the need for relationship that honors the fullness of her body structure, then her body that is alive also recognizes these value messages and responds accordingly. To embrace the idea of embodiment is to acknowledge and respect that the relationship one has with the self, in addition to intentional energy exchange, conversation, behaviors, and thoughts, will inform the state of one's body existence.[16] African American clergy women—who have certainly found themselves the objects of considerable stress, violence, discrimination, sexism, and related oppressive acts—might explore an important question here. When reaction to injustices has been to fight with the same destructive and imbalanced energy that incites oppression, have African American clergy women cut themselves off from or unknowingly disregarded the power of their unique essence? Have they cut themselves off from creativity, spiritual gifting, and healing that may have a direct impact on physical health manifestations within their body?

It appears that African American clergy women on occasion have interpreted the burden of the call through stereotypical and cultural messages. The particular messages I speak of have at times reinforced what I spoke of earlier—sacrificial behavior for the sake of the other while neglecting the impact of stress related issues on their bodies. Consequently, common results are unfortunately negative physical health outcomes, limited availability to those they serve, and permanent absence due to irreparable damage within her body.

Dr. Chanequa Walker-Barnes's notion of the Strong Black Woman (SBW) has been a valuable resource in conversations related to this challenge.[17] For African American clergy women, an understanding that the strength they depend on to sustain them can also contain the problem that possibly weakens them will continue to be an important factor in any work

---

16. See Barratt, *Emergence of Somatic Psychology*, 21, where he defines "embodiment" as the experience of having shape or containment of the self within the body inclusive of empathetic attunement to the internal experience that establishes a reference point for self-reflection and self-attunement.

17. See Walker-Barnes, *Too Heavy a Yoke*, 6–7, where she discusses legacy of the term StrongBlackWoman and the nomenclature used over the years to describe what she believes ultimately is at its common core. The StrongBlackWoman is an adaptive response by Black women that, on one hand, enables them to cope with the very real pressures of their lives, yet, on the other, places them at heightened risk for physical and psychological distress.

developing aspects of relevant healing practices. We will look more intently at physical manifestations that continue to threaten women through early embodied messages and experiences imposed upon their psyche, either consciously or unconsciously, and what reparative measures and ritual practices might help to shape, improve, prevent, positively affect, and/or heal revealed physical conditions.

2

Toward an Understanding of Body-Mind Connection

IN A SOCIETY THAT increasingly demands attention to synthetic means of relating (connecting) and deems technological advancement the pinnacle of success and progress, we are often forced to consider what we have relied upon concerning our identity and self-understanding in light of such externally focused and dis-embodied means of existing. Our fundamental exploration of what it means to be human in a society that we hope encourages healthy, civilized, and peaceful interaction with one another has often been reflected upon in the trusted spaces of psycho-therapeutic work in pursuit of psychological healing. In recent history, new disciplines helped to expand and broaden an understanding of what was needed in reflection of our humanity given current relational realities. Barnaby Barratt, a psychoanalyst and senior research fellow at the University of Cape Town, asserts the following: "These newly forming disciplines like somatic psychology[1] and bodymind therapy[2] within the human sciences,

---

1. See Barratt, *Emergence of Somatic Psychology*, 21, where he defines somatic psychology as the psychology of the body, a discipline that focuses on the lived experience of embodiment as human beings and that recognizes this experience as the foundation and origination of all our experiential potential. It is a psychology "of" the body distinct from a focus "about" the body.

2. Barratt, *Emergence of Somatic Psychology*, 2. Barratt defines BodyMind therapy as healing practice that is grounded on the wisdom of the body and guided by the knowledge and the vision of somatic psychology.

are not without precedence. They, along with a significant group of healing practices considered both newly emerging and re-emergent are being remembered or rediscovered."[3] In his book *The Emergence of Somatic Psychology and BodyMind Therapy,* Barratt examines the body and mind as an integrated whole and offers a different way of looking at our therapeutic efforts, particularly how consciousness interfaces with human experience. He includes the energy sciences, ancient holistic disciplines, and various psychotherapeutic foci and draws upon phenomenology, depth psychology, and neuroscience to inform his writing. This innovative work was especially useful in helping to clarify the progression of thought within the field of psychology on therapies that have the potential to revolutionize the next century. As advancements are made in technology and health sciences, alternate ways of doing therapy were being considered, especially where it concerns connectivity between mind and body.

In another resource, *The Body Has a Mind of Its Own*, Sandra and Matthew Blakeslee present research and scientific study toward an even greater understanding of what can be learned about the "Embodied Brain and Body Map" or "Mandala." They introduce a significant discussion about the importance of recognizing our agency in community with our bodies, a very critical factor (as I named in the introduction of this book), when the body has so often been taken from central focus. In their work they highlight the importance of recognizing our agency in community with our bodies due to messages of reliance on "spirit" alone, especially in religious circles. The authors stress that an awareness that the body and brain exist for each other is key.[4] Blakeslee and Blakeslee offer insight into what our bodies are subject to despite our active awareness. The following quotation focuses this point:

> The idea that your brain maps chart not only your body, but the space around your body, that these maps expand and contract to include everyday objects, and even that these maps can be shaped by the culture you grow up in, is very new to science. Research now shows that your brain is teeming with body maps—maps of your body's surface, its musculature, its intentions, its potential for action and intentions of other people around you.[5]

---

3. Barratt, *Emergence of Somatic Psychology*, 1.
4. Blakeslee and Blakeslee, *Body Has a Mind of Its Own*, 12.
5. Blakeslee and Blakeslee, *Body Has a Mind of Its Own*, 12–13.

Our Bodies Are Alive

A practical example of this dynamic might be considered when people occasionally approach a structure, such as a low bridge or tunnel, and find themselves compensating with their bodies to make more space in order to clear the structure; the space around them has been mapped to the brain as a part of them. In athletics, the idea of perfecting a particular technique or movement may be informed by the mapping of an object used to compete in a sport. It is as becoming fluent with a bat or tennis racquet as an extension of the arm or a basketball becoming part of the whole body in motion can be felt keenly in connection or relation to a desired goal, which has also been mapped. The term for this invisible volume of space is what neuroscientists call "peripersonal space."[6]

They further illuminate that maps are not static but able to adjust over time without our full knowledge of it. It is a fascinating act of our unconscious and conscious activity as well as an informative body of knowledge about the evolutionary outcomes humans have experienced over time. Being more attentive to ourselves in this manner, as will be necessary in any healing model or approach, has weighty implications for transforming behaviors and the wellness of African American clergy women. When exploring what particularly becomes a part of our mapping experience in the space within and beyond our bodies, it is important to not only consider inanimate objects but our experiences with people, our history, and present contexts, as referenced in the remainder of this quote:

> These body centered maps are profoundly plastic—capable of significant reorganization in response to damage, experience, or practice. Formed early in life, they mature with experience and then continue to change, albeit less rapidly, for the rest of our life. Yet, despite how central these maps are to your being, you are only glancingly aware of your own embodiment most of the time, let alone the fact that its parameters are constantly changing and adapting, minute by minute, and year after year. The constant activity of your body maps is so seamless, so automatic, so fluid and ingrained, that you don't even recognize it's happening, much less that it poses an absorbing scientific puzzle that is spawning fascinating insights into human nature, health, learning, our evolutionary past, and cybernetically enhanced future.[7]

---

6. Blakeslee and Blakeslee, *Body Has a Mind of Its Own*, 3.
7. Blakeslee and Blakeslee, *Body Has a Mind of Its Own*, 3.

Toward an Understanding of Body-Mind Connection

David W. Krueger takes us back to look at early-life development and how our sense of the body forms and is informed. In his book *Integrating Body Self and Psychological Self: Creating a New Story in Psychoanalysis and Psychotherapy*, the body self and somatic experience-representation is examined through exploration of the idea that psychoanalysis "perhaps has left these behind in the idealization of cognition, assuming the body as developmentally differentiated, Oedipal, and verbally accessible; assumptions that may stem from Freud's consistent alignment of the body with the unconscious relegating it to metaphor and therefore not directly linked to the sensory or affective experience of the moment."[3] Krueger is wise to insist on respect for the body and its worthiness to be situated not in the background or in afterthought but rather essentially in the foreground for integrative thinking about health. He progressively builds upon these ideas through writings he labels "developmental origins of the body-self," "understanding body disruptions," "gender identification within the body," "the mind-brain-psyche-body influence on each other," "memory and trauma," and "somatic symptoms inclusive of conversion, psychosomatic, somatic action and somatic memories." Krueger's work is a good pairing with similar ideas espoused by Dr. Edward Wimberly in *Recalling Our Own Stories*, particularly around the notion of re-authoring our stories. Krueger also speaks of the importance of "Creating a New Story: Re-Transcripting the Mindbrain," wherein he highlights the importance of a patient and analyst becoming coauthors of a new story, creating meaning that allows a growing distinctness of the interwoven new and old stories. In this regard, exploring and/or making use of models that aid in altering embedded scripts located within the body was useful in my work of crafting and creating a framework housing embodied healing and liberative approaches for African American clergy women.

When crafting and subsequently utilizing a framework for these approaches, indigenous spiritual practices play a significant role. Roy Moodley and William West's *Integrating Traditional Healing Practices into Counseling and Psychotherapy* brings together highly qualified practitioners from various areas of expertise and experience with clients as a way to discuss integrative approaches to care and healing that have always existed in many indigenous cultures and have forced the field of psychotherapy to take a respectful look at what traditional healing practices have to offer. They speak of the integration of traditional and indigenous healing for

---

8. Krueger, *Integrating Body Self and Psychological Self*, xi.

clients seeking relevant cultural metaphors, symbols, and archetypes that may be outside of the parameters of Western counseling and psychotherapy but have proven to be effective healing tools as evidenced in several client outcomes.[9] The effort to highlight the rich healing traditions of cultures from around the globe and the possibility of these working together for the empowerment and healing of those we serve in our field was a significant contribution to this book.

The Community of Self (Revised) by African American psychologist Na'im Akbar is also a valuable point of reference and a significant contributor to the topic of body communication and relationship. I appreciate that he gives attention to the cultural "space" within one's literal mind-body community and offers practical conceptions that are useful in the topic of self-literacy and the creation of a practical healing model. Akbar suggests that one is not fully competent and aware until one explores in depth that aspect of culture within the self. His work emphasizes the need to relate and communicate authentically with all aspects of our bodies and minds as units for optimal health outcomes. He also suggests that knowledge of the self is the key to human power and effectiveness and offers a synthesis of psychology, spirituality, religion, sociology, and cultural studies to explore deeper understandings about the internal organization of the body's community. Important in this process is the direction to evaluate the noise around us and what may hinder the voice of spirit within. I appreciate his specific lens on the trauma African Americans have had to overcome and yet endure, and how communal attitudes and principles help to shape these concepts of self. Dr. Akbar addresses other significant ideas I hold critical related to energetic exchange and its impact on shaping our ways of being and relating with ourselves and others. His section on "Unnatural Mentality," a term pointing to the exploration of some of the root causes of mental illness, particularly those related to religious teachings that have been harmful in some respects, was central when engaging in interviews with African American clergy women who suffered debilitating pain at the hands of the church.

In her book *African American Folk Healing*, womanist theologian Stephanie Mitchem offers insights into varying perspectives of the "Black body" in American culture and its marked influence on generations that have been subject to the imposed imaging of what value their flesh and humanity hold. Mitchem's focus on the African American woman's faith

---

9. Moodley and West, *Integrating Traditional Healing Practices*, xv.

Toward an Understanding of Body-Mind Connection

life grounds her interests in concepts of health, illness, and healing in light of spirituality as well as a path to better understand health practices. Beneficial to this topic is her exploration of non-Western-sanctioned healing practices that look into the culturally derived concepts that Black people have about wellness and how the concepts have evolved, persisted in their relevance, and continued to offer remedies to heal Black minds, bodies, and communities.[10] She draws on historical African perspectives to help inform and remind us of critical resources that have been abandoned in some ways and richly maintained in others. They are views about the body that, if embraced, may aid one in recognizing that human life is understood relationally as part of the interconnected, shared web of the universe. Mitchem reports in a quote from Guerin Montilius a notion that the body is a sight to be revered and proud of in the face of ignorance that would judge external realities while missing the deeply spiritual significance of divine vessels that embody knowledge, love, and communal wisdom, connecting the physical and spiritual world:

> In general, African understandings of the body perceive it "as the agent of concrete totality, radical identity, and ontological unity of the human being." It follows, then, that spiritual values and meanings are reflected in the body itself. One expression of this idea is that differently shaped bodies, sometimes deemed a deformity in Western eyes, might instead be considered spiritually meaningful, depending on African tradition. The body signals something about the spiritual life, encompassing the personal, familial, and communal in the present moment. More than that, the body connects the person to the ancestors and a new birth in a family may signal the return of an ancestral spirit.[11]

Such regard for the body is precisely what I set out to reinforce in a healing practice; a regard that reveals the extent to which some of the lived experiences of African American clergy women either reinforced regard for the body or a lack thereof. I repeat here that the perceived relationship one has with the self significantly determines one's state of function and health. To imagine it as intricately connected to unexplored levels within should yield revolutionary ways of thinking about our interaction not only with ourselves but also with others.

---

10. Mitchem, *African American Folk Healing*, 3.
11. Mitchem, *African American Folk Healing*, 35.

3

A Necessary Path

Unearthing Our Body Narratives

WOMANIST THOUGHT GROUNDS THIS work and brings a lens of sensitivity not only to the plight of Black women but also to women everywhere who are marginalized and relegated to the fringes of society. Womanist theologian Stephanie Mitchem asserts that "womanism resonates with the traditions of African American oral culture and draws upon religious resources that aide in the process of defining, naming, shaping, responding to, and otherwise creating the rich dimensions of African American women's religious lives."[1] Mitchem, following Deloris Williams, clarifies a bit more of what lies at the core of relevant insights on womanist thought related to the topic of healing and wellness:

> Womanist theology challenges all oppressive forces impeding Black woman's struggle for survival and for the development of a positive, productive, quality of life conducive to women's and the families' freedom and well-being. Womanist theology opposes all oppression based on race, sex, class, sexual preference, physical disability and caste.... Womanist theology... can branch off in its own direction, introducing new issues and constructing new analytical categories.[2]

---

1. Mitchem, *Introducing Womanist Theology*, 81.
2. Mitchem, *Introducing Womanist Theology*, 81.

As she analyzes the interconnecting oppressions of race, class, and gender, Mitchem further asserts that womanist theology is grounded in experience and faith. To this list I emphasize a need for inclusion of issues that affect the body related to these interconnecting factors.

The path toward "unearthing body narratives" and crafting a relevant healing model included consideration of psychotherapeutic models that address identity formation and developmental phases. Along with cultural and social factors, these theoretical concepts became appropriate partners when devising a survey instrument I utilized for qualitative interviews with willing participants on the journey toward meaningful healing practices. Object relations and family systems theories in particular were used with the intent to explore personal views African American clergy women held about their self-body relationship at distinct periods of life, beginning in childhood through to adulthood. The following is a summary of that design and process.

I interviewed ten African American clergy women by recording their sacred stories of relationality to their bodies and the impact on their bodies. Their call to leadership and the care of others in ministry was also a major point of focus. The unique experiences of these clergy women who offered their narratives may point toward the experiences of larger groups of women in similar circumstances.

During interviews my goal was to hear the narratives of participants and to listen for their interpretation of those experiences. Situating African American clergy women as subjects narrating and analyzing their own experience positioned them as primary sources in the development of a knowledge base for this exploration. Participants had the opportunity to share old and new insights in their experiences during the interview process.

A personal invitation was extended to fifteen African American clergy woman including womanist theologians, scholars, professors, pastors, chaplains, and those who identify as spiritual practitioners in other capacities. Ten women from among those invited responded affirmatively. It was my intention to secure at least ten African American clergy women who had been in active ministry at least fifteen years, which was the only criteria other than being of African descent, clergy, and a woman. The number ten was decided based on my use of a qualitative interview method that would garner not only significant information about individual experiences but also commonalities among participants related to their history, behaviors, health outcomes, and healing practices. I was additionally interested in exploring the intricacies of African American clergy women's sacred stories related to their bodies and health outcomes as well as the wealth of personal data that would be potentially generated.

My goal in setting criteria for fifteen years of ministry was to help ensure that participants held leadership experience in the act of caring for others over a substantial period of time. In addition, reflection over their own development and evolution in ministry was a rich source from which they could draw. Though not pre-determined or initially requested, the age of participants seemed to be impacted by the criteria of having a fifteen-year minimum in ministry. Consequently, the ages of participants ranged between forty-five and sixty-five. Birth places of participants spanned south- and mid-western regions of the United States to southern, northern, and eastern regions. All but one participant was seminary educated. All were professionals with a bachelor's degree or higher and employed in some capacity within churches, primary schools, universities, seminaries, hospitals, the US military, and/or other specialty ministries. All but two of the participants held ordination credentials as pastor/elder, while the others were licensed for ministry in their denominations. Fifty percent of the participants were married, and the others were either divorced or never married.

In addition to what has already been stated, another goal was to gain insight into African American clergy women's views of their relationship with their bodies and how they understand, if any, correlations to health outcomes in connection with a particular view and/or way of relating. The way in which African American clergy women image and relate to their body as well as the impact of historical messages that have been passed from generations was explored in a manner that supported conversation that was unforced, organic in nature, and respectful of each individual's offering.

I was met with a great deal of interest and curiosity to explore the following questions which held their experiences center. Below is the list of questions utilized and that became a significant survey instrument in this healing work:

Qualitative Interview Questions

1. *What were early messages you received about your body?*
2. *How would you describe your relationship with your body (a) in your youth, (b) in young adulthood, and (c) currently?*

3. *How would you describe what you are most passionate about addressing in ministry (a) in your youth, (b) in young adulthood, and (c) currently?*
4. *What are the greatest challenges you feel African American clergy women face?*
5. *What models did and do you draw from to engage pastoral ministry (not limited to church)?*
6. *How do you feel that model/approach has worked for you? What impact would you say that model/approach has had or is having on your body?*
7. *Have you experienced negative health outcomes since adulthood?*
8. *Are there rituals you engage as part of a healing practice?*

These questions stimulated reflective dialogue that aided in unearthing critical insight into the participant's processes of growing self-identification and relationship/non-relationship with their bodies and subsequent associated outcomes. A brief explanation of the rationale for each of the questions follows:

Questions-Survey Instrument

1. *What were early messages you received about your body?*
2. *How would you describe your relationship with your body (a) in your youth, (b) in young adulthood, and (c) currently?*

Many developmental, psychoanalytic, and family systems theories assert that primary relationships and early life experiences hold significant influence on self-imaging and self-understanding. From these we learn that we are socially and culturally shaped by elements of our environments and relationships and will amass embedded messages likely to remain affixed within our minds and bodies until new information is presented and received on some level. It was my intent to spark childhood memories that would lay a foundation for the interview conversation that was rooted in the participant's expressed experience. Each subsequent question built on the previous, revealing a type of sequential conjuring of memories depicting developmental phases of life and maturing stages of understanding related to how the participant interfaced with her body.

3. *How would you describe what you were most passionate about addressing in ministry (a) in your youth, (b) in young adulthood, and (c) currently?*

Object relations and sociocultural theories support notions of awareness that an individual's behaviors can be significantly affected by their surroundings, social factors, and cultural factors. These schools of thought also support the idea that passion and interest are formulated relationally and through the mirroring of others in the community.

Jungian psychology expounds upon this point through a teleological view of life wherein a sense of purpose is being developed and shaped by beckoning goals that will ultimately lead to integration of and harmony with the self.[3] For Jung, this process is one of individuation that is a reconciling of opposites within a person. Jung importantly also regards humans' need for religion and for God as an inherent drive directed toward self-fulfillment and, ultimately, clarity of purpose.[4] All of these promulgate thought that one will lean toward a certain path unless primary relationships and experiences steer them elsewhere and otherwise nurture pseudo interests—*interests originating from those primary authority figures rather than the person*—in order to fulfill another's desires. It was my intent with participants to explore whether they recognized particular interests and gifts from primary years in life and, if so, where that interest may have originated or been rooted. Exploration of their maturational process included an assessment of how they made meaning of their interest at different phases of life, how it shifted (or not), and how they ultimately came to focus as intently on their current ministry path. My goal also included helping to unearth awareness about developmental processes and significant influences from relationships that may have shaped particular ministry function. Conditions such as post-traumatic stress or unresolved grief can manifest unhealed pain from earlier periods that may reveal correlations to particular choices later in life. At times those choices—in this case, ministry choices—are based upon efforts to heal pain. An understanding of this dynamic in the life of the participants I interviewed may have offered insight into particular types of energy that remained in their body to the present day. These questions would also serve to build a foundation for

---

3. Monte, *Beneath the Mask*, 441.
4. Monte, *Beneath the Mask*, 441.

future dialogue connected to the call narrative of each clergy woman and the challenges that would eventually surface for them.

4. *What are the greatest challenges you feel African American clergy women face?*

Identifying what is most challenging for clergy women further unearthed particular themes and patterns of thought held by participants. Exploring this area would help to reveal where and how beliefs and struggles about African American clergy women originated, how they manifested, and/or how related energy came to be held within their body in some manner. The way in which challenges are viewed might give insight into how the participant meets struggle and how their bodies might absorb the struggle in particular ways. Pain, resentment, joy, or any number of emotions may surface and become a resource for additional information about motivators or barriers to ministry and health. I began to listen for messages that may have had connections to earlier unhealed pain or imposed ministry functions early in life.

5. *What models did and do you draw from to engage pastoral ministry (not limited to the church)?*

6. *How do you feel that model/approach has worked for you? What impact would you say that model/approach has had or is having on your body?*

As mentioned above, each question builds upon previous investigation. A continuation of reflection, unearthing, and assessment was the goal here. Specifics lie in evaluating and revisiting mirroring behaviors drawn from members of our community, mentors, ministers, and other role models that could have proven productive or counter-productive. Greater awareness of developmental processes and significant influences from relationships that may have shaped particular ministry function remained significant. An understanding of this dynamic in the life of the participants I interviewed offered insight into particular types of energetic forces that may have remained in their body to present day. If mentoring relationships resulted in inauthentic function, over-function, or "other focus" as a general rule, then the possibility of greater struggle and consequently greater negative health outcomes may have been increased. Investigation of this question was to assess whether a betrayal of self and that which is genuinely the path of the participant could have eventually become a source of body trauma and negative health outcomes.

7. *Have you experienced negative health outcomes since adulthood?*

Exploring correlation between early messages and subsequent negative health outcomes was the focus of this question. It was envisaged that responses to this question could possibly enable documentation of negative health outcomes for future public health practice.

8. *Are there rituals you engage as part of a healing practice?*

It has been my observation that many people use spiritual practices to address health outcomes. Unfortunately, it occurs far too often after they have received news of a health challenge or negative health outcome. Historically, African American culture has been rich in healing practices related to the use of herbs, natural remedies, retained indigenous practices for healing, and more. I was interested to explore whether participants had used such practices for routine health or if only when challenged. Moreover, I wished to assess the correlation between routine spiritual practice and health outcomes.

Research questions sparked rich and profound dialogue, reaching considerably beyond the question. The experience evoked curiosity, surprise, tears, pain, and deep emotional reactions to memories forgotten or not even considered. The dialogue at times also became an awakening to connections that were even unclear just moments prior. The significance of the first and second questions seemed to generate fascination and somewhat disarming effects. Most importantly, the questions called for respect and reverence of participants and their bodies: the focus of which placed them at the center of the dialogue wherein affirmation rather than judgment stood as the framework for engagement. Unfortunately, according to participants, it is a framework often lacking in the lives of many Black women. Finally, conducive spaces, honored time, privacy, and confidence that therapeutic assistance was available should any part of the interview trigger unmanageable distressing responses allowed for authentic, intimate, and healing experiences, according to participants.

In the next section, I introduce the ten research participants and share portions of their narratives through excerpts from individual qualitative interviews. A short profile of each participant follows with an understanding that each identifies as a woman of African descent—a few have mixed heritage from Caribbean and Native American culture. The following are pseudonyms I gave to each of the participants in order to preserve anonymity: Wanda, Violet, Autumn, Frankie, Spirit, Jane, Sharon, Yvette, Lex, and Rachael.[5]

Wanda is a fifty-two-year-old ordained Protestant clergyperson who serves as co-pastor at a successful and thriving church where she is well-respected and loved. She also serves as a professional in a hospital institution where she provides pastoral care. Wanda holds leadership roles within her vocational organization. She is a mother of one son and a wife within her second marriage. In addition, she is actively engaged within her community and is service-oriented. Wanda reports having experienced migraine headaches and high blood pressure on rare occasions. These seem to be situational rather than chronic.

Violet is a fifty-six-year-old ordained Protestant clergyperson who is very active in her denomination and church. She has pastored a congregation and now works professionally in a hospital institution providing pastoral care. She serves in leadership roles within her professional organization, has never been married, and has no children. Violet reports being a cancer survivor over many years.

Autumn is a sixty-year-old Protestant pastor of a large successful church and ministry. She is active in her local community as well as nationally and globally. She serves as a mentor for others in pastoral ministry, is well respected, and is recognized for her professional leadership and accomplishments. She has never been married and has no children. Autumn reports having experienced situational high blood pressure.

Frankie is a forty-five-year-old ordained Protestant clergy and academic scholar. She holds leadership roles in her church and community and advocates social justice issues as well as African-centered values. She travels to preach and is an adjunct professor. Frankie is married with three children. She reports having experienced significant health challenges related to liver and kidney function and has also been intentional about improving her health related to the impact of excess weight.

---

5. All names have been changed to protect the identity of participants in this research study. Additionally, names of identifying cities, institutions, and friends or relatives of participants have been omitted to ensure anonymity.

Spirit is a forty-six-year-old Protestant pastor of a successful church and is an academic scholar. She serves in leadership roles within the institution where she works and travels nationally to preach. She champions social justice issues as well as African-centered values. She is well-respected for her many gifts and accomplishments. Spirit has never been married and has no children. She reports neurological and degenerative conditions that can impact various movement and other functions at times.

Jane is a fifty-four-year-old ordained Protestant clergyperson who works as an institutional chaplain. She holds leadership roles both in her institution and in her professional organization where she is very well respected. She preaches and is very active in pastoral care. Jane is married with one child. Jane reports having had a hysterectomy and is managing high blood pressure that surfaces on occasion.

Sharon is a sixty-one-year-old ordained Protestant clergyperson who is the co-pastor of a successful church. She has worked in healthcare previously as a clinician and then as a chaplain. She is very active in her denomination and well respected for her leadership. Sharon is divorced and has two adult children. Sharon reports that she is a cancer survivor and often experiences many other limiting physical conditions due to her age, like arthritis and heartburn.

Yvette is a fifty-eight-year-old ordained Protestant clergyperson who works as an institutional chaplain. She holds leadership roles in her church as well as in her professional organization where she is very well respected. Yvette is very active in pastoral care and is service oriented in her community. She is divorced and has two adult children. Yvette reports being a cancer survivor.

Lex is a forty-nine-year-old licensed Protestant minister at a large successful church. She holds leadership roles within that community as well as the community at large. She champions children and family wellness and works within the academic setting where she teaches and is engaged with youth. Lex is married with one child. Lex reports having diabetes and other conditions possibly impacted by excess weight that she is working to decrease.

A Necessary Path

Rachael is a fifty-year-old ordained protestant clergyperson and academic scholar. She serves in leadership roles within the academic institution in which she works and travels nationally to preach, present papers, and engage mission work. She champions social justice issues as well as African-centered values. She is well-respected for her gifts and accomplishments. Rachael reports having never been seriously ill. She is watching cholesterol numbers that show elevation on occasion.

4

African American Clergy Women Narrating Their Sacred Stories

What were early messages you received about your body?

How would you describe your relationship with your body—in your youth, young adulthood, and currently?

Wanda—"*I grew up kind of feeling ashamed of my body. . . . We had to keep it covered at all times. . . . I never saw my mother's body either. She made it so that neither of us could see each other, so I thought something was wrong with my body.*"

Violet—"*You had to sit with your legs closed, be clean and not put yourself out there for people to notice or be drawn to you.*"

Autumn—"*I was too Black, too skinny, too tall; I couldn't wear bright colors . . . didn't know to value it, I didn't value it in terms of taking care of myself. I did not cherish it because those were not the kind of messages I received. The book, Our Bodies Our Selves, helped me to become more aware of my body during the time when I went to college.*"

Frankie—"It was through the community that I knew I had a body because attention was drawn to it when me and friends moved our bodies in certain ways and were reprimanded from community women. Another message was that the body was vulnerable and men could do something to it. I got that from watching my mother being physically abused by men. Pentecostal church experience in college caused dissonance when messages about the flesh being bad or negative began to surface. Holiness was connected to body restrictions, abstaining from sex—gave impression that body was now 'bad,' which was not the case in my experience before. I began praying to bring the body under subjection; the body became an enemy I needed to control."

Spirit—"My behind was big, do not have sex it's only for marriage, no touching yourself, lighter skin was preferred over darker skin, I was sort of in the middle, not too much of either."

Jane—"Your body really wasn't discussed, so I grew up with a negative perspective about womanhood. . . . The body in terms of physicality was considered an object rather than your person. Around ten years old, I did my own reading biblically—I learned that my body was the temple of God and that it was holy and sacred and should be treated with respect. From parents—you just didn't talk about the body. It was usually equated with sex, so you just didn't."

Sharon—"That I was freckled and because my grandmother was disappointed with them she tried to get rid of them. . . . My other grandmother was always worried about the kitchen in the back of my head. . . . That girls should walk straight, hold hands together properly, curtsy when you speak, cross your ankles—be proper."

Yvette—"Being one of the darkest girls in my first grade class—I got a lot of teasing."

Lex—"That your body was a private place, with private areas, parts that no one was to touch and you couldn't ask questions. . . . There was no explanation about breasts, puberty, or menstrual cycle so I had to learn on my own and it was scary."

Rachael—"That I shouldn't defile my body or be engaged in sex while young. There was concern about shame and reputation. . . . Expectation was that we would take care of our bodies, eat vegetables, take our cod liver oil and castor oil so that we would stay healthy because

Our Bodies Are Alive

the body needed to be well in order to help support work on the farm and family. . . . The body was useful and you needed to be doing something productive with it, not be slothful."[1]

THE ABOVE STATEMENTS ARE excerpts from answers to the research question, "What were early messages you received about your body?" Many of the statements can be considered remnants of the collective history of African-descent persons and the legacy associated with the relation or lack thereof to the body—vestiges that, though old, remain significantly influential even in the present day. Unfortunately, many of these influences are rooted in painful history wherein Black bodies were commodified and owned by those other than the one whose spirit dwelled within that body. Stephanie Mitchem reminds us of this reality through certain factors that have disturbingly shaped Black identity over time at the hands of white Americans who chose to define Black bodies for their own purposes. She shares from the writings of Walter Johnson's *Soul by Soul: Life Inside the Antebellum Slave Market*, which discusses the processes by which Black people were turned into labor products:

> The questioning of the humanness of people of color by white Americans was chillingly pragmatic; black bodies, after all, were imported as labor and designated as investment property with no rights to participate in the society of the United States. . . . Gazing, touching, stripping, and analyzing aloud, the buyers read slaves' bodies as if they were coded versions of their own imagined needs—age was longevity, dark skin immunity, a stout trunk stamina, firm muscles production, long fingers rapid motion, firm breasts fecundity, clear skin good character. The purposes that slaveholders projected for slaves' bodies were thus translated into natural properties of those bodies.[2]

A greater understanding of this history is crucial if one is to explore the profound alienation inherent in almost every answer to the question of early thought construction about the body. Coping or survival strategies utilized in an effort to protect the body that at one time was deemed less than human and undeserving of any protection or value offer some context for early foundations of estrangement and even hostility toward the body one may now possess. Embodied thinking and reverent regard for the divine creation of the body has been a foreign concept for far too many

---

1. See Piggue, "African American Clergy Women," 153–55.
2. Johnson, *Soul by Soul*, cited in Mitchem, *African American Folk Healing*, 41.

African American women. It is understandably so, given the traumatic history she has had to endure. At the cellular level, body mapping/memory, somatic psychology, and neuroscientific research substantiate enduring, active, and persistent distress.

Much like the oppressed body referenced in the quotation above, the African American body is often relegated to fringes within the communities of our families and churches and tossed aside to exist as a marginalized entity only to be engaged at a prescribed time by the authority imposing such a directive. In a sense, the body is still owned and controlled externally, thus impacting the intimacy one might develop for their own bodies.

This phenomenon has unfortunately continued over decades, disguised beneath the mask of freedom and the label of strength, but it is dynamically still very much alive and destructive to the health of African American Women. Chanequa Walker-Barns points us toward the resemblance of history in current practices and references related to African American women in the following statements in her book *Too Heavy a Yoke: Black Women and the Burden of Strength*:

> Unfortunately, because Black women's strength has become such a cultural mandate, their suffering is often viewed as normative. And because the StrongBlackWoman bears the burden of strength to an extreme, she often does not recognize the emotional and physical distress that is a result of her stress, but takes it for granted as a normal consequence of life. In essence, she has developed an extraordinary capacity for "walking with broken feet," often unaware that she is in pain. Further, when she does become aware of her distress, she is unlikely to attribute it to role strain and is prone to associate it with weakness and insufficiency in meeting the demands that life has placed upon her. Thus, strength becomes a double-edged sword: women who suffer emotional and/or physical breakdowns as a result of repressing and suppressing stress responses believe that the solution is greater repression and suppression![3]

Maladaptive behaviors within our communities have continued to perpetuate harsh and irreverent views of the African American female body and have sadly been adopted as an expected lot in life by others, but most significantly by African American women who have been disembodied for years. Walker-Barnes references Beauboeuf-Lafontant in *Behind the Mask*

---

3. Walker-Barnes, *Too Heavy a Yoke*, 23.

as she continues to help challenge the dangers of disembodied thinking and its impact on the physical health of Black women:

> Eventually, the combined effect of role strain and poor self-care results in the embodiment of stress. Embodiment is a central concept in eco-social theory and helps us to understand how stress is translated into health problems. Among StrongBlackWomen, embodiment is the usually unconscious process by which women's bodies become the repositories of the stresses and strains resulting from the personification of a socially constructed role.[4]

As we continue to examine the experiences of African American clergy women in relation to their bodies, listening to their narratives and understanding the challenges that have existed over time may point to some of the early foundational messages rooted in historical institutions of oppression and, as mentioned, socially-constructed ideas that promote disembodiment. The question of how these women directly related to their bodies at different phases of development further built upon the notion of alienation and a lack of self-relationship. Never having been introduced to one of the most essential parts of our being seems unfathomable, yet this has been one of the most prevailing realities for many African American clergy women as expressed in the following interview responses to question number two:

How would you describe your relationship with your body—in your youth, young adulthood, and currently?

Within the responses to follow, much like those from question one, themes of alienation from the body were prevalent. One theme was the internalization of negative thinking about the body from an early age and the absence of dialogue that would normalize awareness, love, and care for the body. Another theme focused on body descriptions, rules, and restrictions associated with how the body was to be handled and/or maintained. A third had to do with caution or warnings about or against sexual activity.

During our time with this question, I found that nine of the ten women experienced having had minimal dialogue with adults pertaining to their relationship with their bodies; half of them being left alone to figure out how to attend to natural female body function such as menstruation and other significant developmental experiences of embodiment. Most of the

---

4. Walker-Barnes, *Too Heavy a Yoke*, 67.

participants became deeply reflective and engaged long moments of silence as they realized what could be unhealthy patterns and what the consequent impact on them had been. Some showed visible disbelief and sadness when thinking back. It appeared to them also that maladaptive behaviors, as spoken of in the previous section, were very much at work. For instance, the following excerpts indicate that behaviors adopted by Black people years ago, possibly rooted in efforts to protect children in an unsafe white-dominated world, may have informed the messages their parents or communities offered them. Some of these adopted strategies were meant to preempt critical and disparaging mockery that could come from the white world or harsh treatment and/or abuse. Consequently, Black parents may have imposed it first in order to "toughen up" their children and prepare them for real-life challenges. Unfortunately, though the intent may have been good, the negative outcomes were at times damaging in their own right[5]:

> [*How would you describe your relationship with your body, in youth, young adulthood, and currently?*]
>
> Wanda—*"It was really detached as a youth. I didn't claim it as my own, if I had that language. I just maintained it. Didn't start cycle until thirteen, but did not have any conversation with my mother about how that was to happen so faked it because others had theirs. I was shocked when it finally came and didn't know what to do: Was sent in bathroom alone to figure out everything."*
>
> Violet—*"I was somewhat ashamed of my body."*
>
> Autumn—*"In my youth I received messages that my body was imperfect and then when I became a young adult, I thought I was ugly. As I matured and was finally getting in touch with things about my body, I began to realize that I really wasn't ugly. I'm not too skinny, men were attracted to me. I then felt a sense of my own sassiness."*[6]

Wanda, Violet, and Autumn's responses also include the adopted strategies of "not becoming too vain" and, especially if in a religious household, being too concerned about the flesh. The role of servant in a racist/sexist society also perpetuated the need to focus on others at the expense of caring for the body. The fear of sexual assault also loomed. Consequently, messages meant to discourage young women in various ways would be imposed by

---

5. hooks, *Sisters of the Yam*, 34–40.
6. See Piggue, "African American Clergy Women," 155–59.

mother's, father's, siblings, and extended family as a way of "caring." The downside of neglecting critical evaluation of historical practices is that they become subject to repetition in future generations. Other participants shared similar experiences of confusion, the witness of abuse and poor role modeling, and never having ever considered that one could actually "have" a relationship with one's body.

> Spirit—"I observed that women's bodies were for men's pleasure and not your own. So, you really didn't have a sense that your body fully belonged to yourself. Introduction to your menstrual cycle, which I was a little late relative to my friends, you kind of learned your body through those experiences and how you negotiate and navigate that in middle school."

> Frankie—"In youth it was abstract-my relationship with my body. Wasn't clear what it could do. Spin the bottle type games suggest doing something with it in adolescence—like a kiss—no real connection with the action. Overall thought—Medically, spiritually and sexually at this stage the body is a great thing."

> Jane—"Not sure I was very conscious about it then, but I was always very skinny."

> Sharon—"As a youth, I tried to be attractive, cute, thin, wear my hair a certain way. Don't remember if I had any particular relationship with my body."

> Lex—"In youth—very awkward and not really knowing about my body. In young adulthood—reading books, finding out what different body parts were and it was just taboo, so you just didn't talk about it. I began to research on own in young adult life. I was always inquisitive about why things work the way they do. My cycle prompted more study. I knew nothing.

> Wondered if I was going to die or bleed to death. The generation before me had the same experience, but didn't do it differently. My PE coach gave me a book."[7]

Rachael was the one participant who received messages that the body was to be cared for and kept in good shape. Though she talks about this directive primarily in light of making sure her body was strong for work and useful

---

7. See Piggue, "African American Clergy Women," 155–59.

for the family's survival, the impact of the messages, as we will hear more in the section on neuroscience, still informed positive interfacing with her body and seemingly positive health outcomes. The argument that messages may not necessarily need context in order to be impactful may apply here as positive regard for the usefulness of the body.

> Rachael—"As a child and young adolescent, I thought I was physically Strong and smarter than my male siblings. So that's one thing I thought about my body. I thought that it was useful. An instrument of who I was. I think that came from growing up on a farm."[8]

Prevalent in the answers as well were descriptions of the body, rules, and restrictions associated with how the body was to be handled and/or maintained. These answers reinforced a sense of the body as an object of scrutiny rather than the body as a loved vessel to embrace, love, and relate to hospitably:

> Wanda—"At a later time when I put socks in my bra, it finally sparked conversation with my mother who affirmed that I was fine the way I was."

> Violet—"In my youth I was very, very skinny. All my siblings were a bit different in body shape than me so I was ashamed of my body as a teenager. One of my brothers laughed at my knees because he saw them as knots . . . so that reinforced that you don't let anyone see that. Going on to college in the first year I gained weight so from young adulthood to mid-adulthood I got attention and could turn heads. But I still wouldn't show my body. The way I dressed would be to cover so nobody really knew my shape because I would wear clothes to camouflage it. . . . But I think I didn't recover from the childhood messages of you had to be a certain way or don't do a certain thing. Interesting thing that it wasn't until after my mom died did I start to become free in my being to appreciate 'Me' as a woman."

> Autumn—"I went through a period of real insecurity from young adulthood to mid. I remember feeling like an ugly duckling and questioning whether I was valued. That came from falling in love and being sexually active. Depending on how a man treated me acceptance/rejection that also played into how I felt about my body."

> Frankie—"Weight—Mother would try to warn against getting heavy, fear was developed about what weight means related to body."

8. See Piggue, "African American Clergy Women," 158.

Our Bodies Are Alive

> Spirit—*"As an early youth, I would have been considered a tomboy, some of this points to gender and embodiment. In youth, physical health was important. Stereotypically, I liked boy stuff. I was athletic, I liked fishing and hunting. I was a dancer as a child as well. So that was always encouraged in some ways."*

> Yvette—*"How I was different? When people point things out to you, I noticed that I had thin legs, a big nose but over all I really didn't think too much about it. My self-awareness—I had a lot of personality; was affirmed by uncle and friend. As I matured, I left for college—my bow legs caught attention. There were incidences after I married. I met my husband in college. After five years of marriage—he had a vile temper and would do name calling and some of the things he would say to me heightened my awareness of who I was—but then I could not look at myself in the mirror."*

> Jane—*"I was always comparing body to sisters, family and friends wishing for more of one thing or another. So body was too skinny, unattractive, etc. As I went to college, and began putting on weight, I got hips and was noticed by others. I became self-conscious then because others were looking and making assessments. Mom has this thing about weight, so comments. It's not about being attractive but healthy."*[9]

For young people in general, body image is a very important part of the developmental process. For African American youth, seeing positive images and likeness to themselves is very necessary as a means of nurturing positive self-image and self-relationship. Too often, comparison and competition reinforce self-contempt and alienation from the body. In the following excerpt, Sharon finds herself lamenting over not having appreciated her body in previous years, and now that it's in pain often, it is difficult for her to think about having a good relationship with her body. She is in fact quite displeased.

> Sharon—*"As a young adult it was more about being pregnant and a parent. I think I came into myself and felt most attractive when I was a young adult. I felt attractive after I had my children. As an older person my relationship is one of disgust—not because it's not attractive but my interest is more about how I feel and my health than what it looks like and I haven't felt well in my body."*[10]

---

9. See Piggue, "African American Clergy Women," 155–59.
10. See Piggue, "African American Clergy Women," 158.

Rachael shares her process of evolving awareness and knowledge of self and celebrates it. Her only confusion or concern came when figuring out how to negotiate the balance between celebrating her physical body and her academic intelligence. There was no one to help translate that for her at the time. The survey question about the impact of early role models reveals more of that process for her. But under this theme, Rachael demonstrates having been able to stay conscientious and caring of her body:

> Rachael—"I thought at one point when I was an early teenager, that I started to become conscious of my body and thought I was too heavy. I guess as I was entering adolescence or teenage years I wanted to look attractive. So, I dressed in ways that I thought were attractive.... I remember my body being attractive by the time I was a senior in high school and flaunting it in purples and lively colors, on into college. I still thought I was smart; though there were not enough messages about how to balance the attention that I got for my body with how intelligent I was. So I was conflicted and confused about that in some ways, probably well into my young adult life. I continued to care for my body. I think the messages I got about what I ate, stayed with me. I think they still do and still have; although I have not been as conscientious.... So in terms of caring for my body now, I think those messages came through and they continue. I appreciate my body and know if I don't care for it, it will not be there for me to be."[11]

To the third theme of this survey instrument, avoidance or strict warnings about sexual activity were common for many. It is also helpful to reference the responses to the first question about "the early messages one received about their body," as they are relevant in this section also. Participants reported having often received little instruction other than simply "not to do it." The taboo nature of the subject of sex informed by some of the historical strategies mentioned previously, in addition to the fear and shame some parents carried themselves about sex, only sparked more interest and curiosity on the part of participants early in their lives. Obedience to the directive without explanation did not garner compliance. Fortunately for some of the participants, they had other leaders like teachers to help them or used informative literature. Others relied on friends who may or may not have had proper information, who served as guides in this area:

---

11. See Piggue, "African American Clergy Women," 158–59.

> Wanda—"*There was no conversation about sex; however, so didn't know anything—had not seen a man's body or barely a woman's body.*"

> Frankie—"*Teen years—was popular, had friends but prided self on not having sex even though some friends did—so used my body as tool to communicate a stance.*"

> Spirit—"*I think young adulthood interestingly was a little more tumultuous for two reasons: One, conservative, evangelical theology renounced the body, so there was not that affirmation of the body. There was that whole Platonic split between body and spirit, the flesh is evil, you were going to hell if you engaged anything to do with the . . . but it was always the gender and sexuality stuff that was a little more disconnected. Introductions to that were conversations with your girlfriends or street friends; that's where you learned stuff, that's where you explored, that's where you would sneak and watch porn and so it didn't come from adults.*"[12]

Because Spirit committed time and study in this area, it was easy for her to draw upon recent knowledge for her reflections. She had come to critically evaluate the messages of those she served in ministry, assessing damage as well as health in individuals who struggled to make sense of the challenges inherent within this topic. She goes on to offer reflections about her continually evolving knowledge and thinking about embodiment:

> Spirit—"*But in terms of gender and sexuality, it was almost always negative outside the context of marriage. So, it wasn't until later in young adulthood in undergrad and grad school that you really start to ask questions about some of those things and become kind of more aware of your body and relationship with it, and start to say 'How the hell can everything be wrong?' Why would God create people with hormones that you don't have anything to do with; you didn't choose it; it's part of your natural evolution and development and then say don't do that? Now that's ridiculous. Masturbation was the biggest sin in young adulthood and youth. It wasn't until later I found out that boys and men don't seem to have any issues with it. They do it days, nights, weekends, and whenever they feel like it and its fine and nobody is reprimanding them for it. But women we have to deal with a lot of guilt and a lot of shame and I distinguish the two because I think for women, guilt can easily turn to shame because it can become a part of your own self-identity and self-definition—it's*

---

12. See Piggue, "African American Clergy Women," 155–59.

not just behavioral anymore which is something you repent for and discharge. It's now who I am and I begin asking questions like what's wrong with me as a person or biologically. So, seminary and of course womanism helped me to get liberated from some conservative evangelical views of my own body and embodiment."

Rachael—*"In terms of relating to my body and my sexuality, I had to learn—had to decipher how to do that. It was difficult and late and challenging and I was fully adult by the time I was comfortable in understanding myself as a sexual person. So, in regard to relating to myself and to my body as, or to sexuality as an element of my embodiment, I don't think that there were places that helped me to navigate and learn about that."*[13]

If we were to consider our definition of disembodied—*separated from or existing without the body*—we might gather that a historical culture of shame and survival originating from trauma associated with years of oppression and control of the body continues in profound ways. These were ways that reinforce the idea that we are somehow not our bodies and that our spirit—the only thing at one time we felt we had control over—was much more important to attend to because it was intangible to those intent on possessing it. We are once again addressing maladaptive behaviors which at one time served the purpose of survival and fortification of the mental strength needed in order to withstand maniacal conduct of hegemonic tyrants.

To become acquainted with and to care for the body was foreign then and has unfortunately remained so. Hospitality that the self deserves has been given away to others while at the same time remaining a very countercultural self-experience for African American clergy women. The following set of participant responses reflect verses I've appreciated from popular artisan India Arie in the song "Private Party."[14] She often uses her craft in dedication to healing and wholeness and thus sings about what many of the participants have spoken. Her song captures not only the unfortunate state of Black women's "disconnect" with their bodies but also the effort made toward awareness and eventual celebration of that body in ways not previously experienced. She suggests that there are options toward healing.

---

13. See Piggue, "African American Clergy Women," 155–59.

14. See Arie, "Private Party," where her message conveys not understanding the origination of disconnection from her body and engaging in conversation with her body toward healing and constructive embodied thought.

Our Bodies Are Alive

Arie's song echoes what some of the participants shared about their evolving introduction to their bodies:

> Yvette—*"It wasn't until later that I started making myself look at me, the whole person, and began to like the person who was there. Self-esteem was something I had to grow because of stigma from early on and the subsequent marriage relationship. That is when it became apparent to me that I had to have some sense of who I was and that if there was something I disliked, I had the option to change it. Currently that is how I would describe it today."*

> Lex—*"Now, I might say I'm more attuned to my body, but still having struggles because I was not taught any touch, exploration, etc. Trying to learn what I like, but it's ok."*

> Wanda—*"Because my spouse was gentle it helped me to get comfortable with my body. Currently I am very attuned to my body and am clear when changes are occurring. Not afraid of it."*

> Violet—*"Currently my relationship with my body is good. I am exercising a lot more now than I ever did. I appreciate my body and I feel freer in me to be a 'Me' and comfortable being a woman. I haven't always been comfortable being a woman and what I mean by that is I hadn't always been comfortable wearing the pretty, frilly things . . . because that would have acknowledged I was a woman and attracted the guys. It's taken me a long time to get to that place and I really do think it had something to do with my mom's death. I think I got some freedom when she died."*

> Spirit—*"I'm claiming who I am and loving that I am fearfully and wonderfully made, knowing that there is nothing ontologically wrong with me. I am now reading writers that help me understand my spirituality in relation to my embodiment."*

> Autumn—*"Once a Christian in young adulthood I fell in love with Psalm 139—it affirmed who I was—'knit in my mother's womb' like the idea of physically being made by design—everything about me is just right. So that today I affirm myself all the time because I am by design. I believe it is important to take care of myself.—Getting plenty of rest, exercise, eating right, not abusing my body. I decided to live celibate. It was a spiritual decision while doing ministry. It has*

meant health—emotionally, physically. . . . No one can play games with my body."[15]

Similar to these participant statements, the message of Arie's "Private Party," conveys the reality that there are Black women who have journeyed through times of disassociation and inauthentic means of relating to their body. She articulates an understanding that constructive embodied thought can lead to some essential healing for those who are out of relationship with the self. Part of that healing begins first with an understanding that separation and disconnection from the body has existed significantly among Black women, rendering their bodies, and therefore themselves, neglected and uncelebrated.

I found that most participants were eventually introduced to a deeper relationship with their bodies, even though delayed. These introductions however came often from outside of the home and/or when illness had become a major part of their lives. The hope is that epiphanies and efforts like those shared by participants and conveyed in Arie's song would become more commonly revered ways of relating to the self: unashamed and easily conversant with the body.

Though one of the later research questions asks about experiences of negative health outcomes, five of ten women shared that physical challenges prompted their growing acquaintance of relationship to their bodies:

> Violet—*"Then because of an illness my body was disfigured. So for about ten years I should have been proud of my body, because it was probably the time in my life when it was close to perfect, but it had been such a difficult time growing up that I hadn't gotten to the point of being able to appreciate my body until the illness showed up. . . . I wasn't ashamed of the disfigurement of the illness because I was grateful to be alive. . . . It seems that I have not had many years of loving my body and I know that I am blessed to be alive because I have been challenged with my illness recurring over the years."*

> Spirit—*"Now as an adult, I think I have a great relationship with my body. I know my body and my body's rhythms. That came through a pretty arduous journey with physical conditions related to stress and hell and unhealthy relationships which worsened the condition along with unhealthy food intake in a certain period of life. But in a strange way and positive way it put me in touch with my body—helped me to understand my body's rhythm and pay attention to pain in my*

---

15. See Piggue, "African American Clergy Women," 155–59.

body in particular kinds of ways. I ignored my body for some time in order to complete school. Now, I am perimenopausal which puts you in touch with your body in other particular kind of ways."

Sharon—*"As an older person, my relationship is one of disgust—not because it's not attractive but my interest is more about how I feel and my health than what it looks like and I haven't felt well in my body. I wish I had appreciated the health that I had because I was very healthy as a young adult. I was a runner and was strong, had excellent memory, my mind was good. I'm seeing myself on the decline as an older person and I am not happy about that at all. So it's a source of aggravation. It hurts—arthritis issues. I can't eat what I want to eat; if I do, it causes discomfort because of a certain medical condition."*

Frankie—*"I had surgery in my youth that prevented me from having fun—unhappy at body restricting life events. Today I have more of an appreciation for the body—more lip service though because I lack enough action that can preserve it. It is an amazing thing to behold, can regenerate and heal itself with correct thoughts and communication. A medical condition that caused other complications within my body has caused me to come into more relationship and intimacy with my body."*

Jane—*"As I've gotten older, I look at my body more through a health lens. My weight often drives how I feel. I am most comfortable at a certain weight. It's more about wanting to be healthy."*[16]

Following these questions, I observed grief on the part of some participants who realized in later years that their bodies had been pretty amazing. They had, in significant ways, missed a window of opportunity to treat her as special as they now realized was possible. Some lamented over the loss, others became more curious, and some became excited to begin nurturing the self immediately, believing that it was never too late.

The experience of disembodiment has for many years been an accepted practice by African American women. Unfortunately, with few models to introduce new information and practices, African American clergy women are still vulnerable and susceptible to the same negative health outcomes spawned by disembodied thinking. As we move toward more embodied thinking and healing, it is important to identify powerful influences that

---

16. See Piggue, "African American Clergy Women," 155–59.

are still very much at work and written in the scripts of our bodies from childhood. We will continue to explore the challenges African American clergy women face in light of the influences in their lives and what has been used over time to aid them in remaining mentally strong, yet physically ill.

Challenges African American Clergy Women Face in Ministry

*What are the greatest challenges you feel
African American clergy women face?*

As I broached the question of challenges faced by African American clergy women, each participant easily dawned a smile—sometimes not really a smile but rather a smirk accompanied by a resounding "humph." One of the women, Rachael, laughed as she began to answer, "You mean what are the challenges African American clergy women face in ministry *besides* being an African American woman and in ministry?"[17] There was a shared sense of knowing among participants related to the complexities inherent within the question. Consequently, there was very little trouble yielding prompt answers.

Research participants who have lent their voice to this study articulate unique and poignant experiences, some of which echo what has been studied and reported within the writing of theorists in the field of pastoral theology and womanist thought. They have lived through it and continue to work toward greater self-literacy, self-relationship, and healing from the impact of such encounters. Nine particular themes emerge from participant responses: (1) various forms of bias against women in ministry; (2) mistrust by others and among one another; (3) lack of support; (4) setting appropriate boundaries; (5) imposed requirements for acceptance in ministry; (6) self-acceptance/being true to oneself; (7) psychological trauma; (8) religious oppression; and (9) theological distortions.

Bias Against Women

The impact of various forms of bias against African American clergy women proved still quite painful for some, and yet for others it was used as a motivator. In particular, motivation was used as a means to more strategically

---

17. Moodley and West, *Integrating Traditional Healing Practices*, xv.

and wisely navigate obstacles in ministry and to avoid being distracted by those who meant ill or imposed their ignorance in harmful ways. The issue of whether a woman can be called to ministry is a common query among those who are a part of certain traditions or hold particular societal expectations. Wanda very pointedly and concisely shares her feelings of how women at times can be their own barriers because of an oppressive history that has taught them not to accept themselves (as women) in ministry:

> Wanda—"*The barrier of ourselves. We've been taught that God does not even call us. No one should have to prove that this is so—even to yourself and your tradition. My family became supportive after they saw it was not a phase.*"[18]

Yvette focused on the impact of male dominance, sexism and disparities that result in the form of negative vocational options:

> Yvette—"*Trying to function in a male dominated situation. Even though women outnumber men in many ways, women are not taken seriously enough to do the jobs that are out there. Women are the last to be considered while men don't seem to have to work as hard.*"[19]

Jane had similar experiences, however noted racial bias that accompanied micro-aggressions present in organized leadership meetings. Leaders seemed to avoid overt racism and/or sexism as it may have revealed behavior the leader would not want to admit. Consequently, respect emerged as the most important issue for Jane:

> Jane—"*Respect. I am a part of a denomination that has only a few churches that embrace women in ministry. So it's respecting that we feel as women that we have been called into this ministry and God has graced us to do this ministry. I am often in leadership experiences in conversation with leaders who are male trying to share my voice. There are white females in that same leadership meeting and it seems they can share. But black women in particular who are there don't often get that same space, so their voices can sometimes be silenced in different ways. So you feel that you are constantly fighting to get your voice heard, to be known, and to be given the same respect as everybody else. So for me it's about respect.*"[20]

---

18. See Piggue, "African American Clergy Women," 162.
19. See Piggue, "African American Clergy Women," 163.
20. See Piggue, "African American Clergy Women," 164.

Sharon and Lex shared similar sentiments about their experiences of gender discrimination against African American clergy women. Sharon was very vocal about the pain these experiences had caused, and Lex shared frustration about the reality of inconsistent treatment of men and women:

> Sharon—*"Voicelessness. I've felt it. You can go to a meeting. You say something and they go on to the next subject and never acknowledge your thought. Encouraging conversation, and then it just goes silent. I believe it happens to us as a Black female. I even feel that African American males are part of that patriarchy as well."*[21]

> Lex—*"Not being accepted by everybody. There is disparity between men and women. It's challenging not feeling as if we have to compete with the man and can focus on what God wants us to do. In society, just being accepted because you are a woman. Seeing the reality of what women really have to deal with is a challenge."*[22]

Mistrust By Others and Among One Another

As Rachael and Violet offered insight about mistrust among clergy women, they were visibly pensive and somewhat disheartened while articulating their experiences. Concern lied in the unfortunate reality of clergy women who find themselves practicing suspicion in relation to one another while at the same time having to fight oppressive forces from outside the circle of clergy sisterhood.

> Rachael—*"Being African American and being female. The greatest challenges? Apart from those two obvious ones, I think everything does stem from those two; I think that the miscommunications, the skepticism, the distrust, of African American clergy women, of each other, and of African American clergy women by others. I think they are all connected to stereotypes that come from race—that are racial engendered. And I don't—it's like a really, really, really vicious cycle."*[23]

Violet spoke about the lack of acceptance by other women for women in ministry, which she deemed equally as problematic on the psyche as men's rejection:

---

21. See Piggue, "African American Clergy Women," 164.
22. See Piggue, "African American Clergy Women," 164.
23. See Piggue, "African American Clergy Women," 164.

> Violet—"*Another thing we face is ostracism by men and women. I think that there are as many women who don't want us in the pulpit as there are men. And I'm not angry about that because I think it goes back to their socialization and what they were raised to believe. So they are living out of their own faith, but they also then are keeping people out and minimizing the opportunity to receive messages that come in a different package.*"[24]

Imposed Requirements for Acceptance into Ministry

In each of her responses, Autumn, an experienced minister and pastor, offered wisdom and clarity to help illustrate not only an understanding of the challenges she had faced but of the lessons she had garnered and how she has made use of them for healing and growth. She had this to share related to measuring up to imposed invisible standards, and having to be better than "others" who in reality were allowed much more space not to be their best:

> Autumn—"*Expectation that we have to be ten times better than the best. Now remember, you are the colored girl here; you are not allowed the same mistakes!*"[25]

In a different manner, Violet speaks of having to be overly mindful of how she comes across in the pulpit and what is appropriate for women and their attractiveness in ministry. She notes that early messages from her upbringing are still very much in play in the message of meeting unspoken standards about what is most "acceptable" in various contexts. Sociocultural dictates from early history related to presenting herself appropriately and managing her sexuality as an attractive woman still seemed to highly govern her sense of self as a clergy leader:

> Violet—"*I think as women when we are in the pulpit though—in talking about the body—we have to be conscious of the message that we send with our body; because everybody in the church aren't Christian and they are not there just to get the message. And preaching is a powerful—what's the word . . . But there is a lot of power contained in the preacher and we add this sexual power and attractiveness of a woman—you have to be mindful of that when you are preaching and how you present yourself and how you dress. I love wearing a robe because it's easy and there are very attractive robes,*

---

24. See Piggue, "African American Clergy Women," 162.
25. See Piggue, "African American Clergy Women," 163.

African American Clergy Women Narrating Their Sacred Stories

> *so I would say wear the attractive robe, but wear the robe. People can get distracted and women talk with their hands a lot and there is a sensual-ness with some people and their hands so you know there are still things we need to be aware of. And I think that all goes back to my upbringing of being mindful of how I presented myself as a person, as a woman, as a girl. It carries itself out today as a preacher, pastor, pastoral care giver."*[26]

Setting Appropriate Boundaries

Autumn and Spirit recognize the necessity of setting appropriate and healthy boundaries, which they know is often poorly managed among clergy women. They were clear that most have been taught to care for others without balance for themselves. Autumn captures in her response one of the factors this dissertation investigates, which is that inattention to this area can leave one ill or permanently absent due to death:

> Autumn—*"Everybody really does depend on us and pulls on us and as women, symbolically we have breast and people want to suck the breast and they often suck us dry. We don't set boundaries—we either don't know how, or refuse to say no. That's a very difficult thing for us—that's a real challenge, And if we don't fall into any of those above, then you find yourself challenged with psychological, emotional or physiological issues—stress being number one. You burn out or walk away, or quit, or you die; if not physically, then spiritually."*[27]

Spirit spoke very personally about the impact of her lack of boundary setting and the impact on her body, especially after experiencing debilitating physical illness:

> Spirit—*"I don't know what that stress did to me physiologically. . . . I have to reach to divest myself of this kind of stress. So stress—embodied—one might want to overeat, not exercise, etc."*[28]

---

26. See Piggue, "African American Clergy Women," 162.
27. See Piggue, "African American Clergy Women," 163.
28. See Piggue, "African American Clergy Women," 163.

Lack of Support

Spirit also speaks to issues related to African American women supporting one another (or the lack thereof) and our need for help in this area. It was my impression from dialogue with most research participants that support and viable numbers of female authority figures within religious institutions had not been readily available. Consequently, the practice of not reaching out to new clergy leaders seemed to continue, becoming her experience as well:

> Spirit—*"Finding genuine support is an ongoing issue. Just because women are pastoring and ordained, everything is still not ok. Sexism, patriarchy still prevalent and can impact the way even black clergy women do to one another. In and out of marriage are challenges in relationships. Courage is a challenge. Taking leaps of faith and at the end of the day, backlash will come to me. Not a lot of people can do what I do."*[29]

Violet's story is one that also illuminates the struggle of acceptance by those within her family and with whom she holds very close and dear relationships:

> Violet—*"When I went into the ministry, I asked my mom what she thought because she was from a denomination that didn't believe in women ministers. She responded, 'God can use women just as good as God can use a man.' She was pretty forward thinking for way back then. My dad said he was fine with it the first year. Well, I don't think women should pastor, you all can preach but I don't think you should pastor. So someone in his denomination got to him and said that women are not supposed to tell men what to do. That was the difference in the pastor and preacher. A pastor tells people what to do differently than a preacher. So my father and I decided to respect each other's position on that even until today. But he would come to hear me preach. So I think a big challenge is, how do we help people understand that the message can come through us?"*[30]

Self Acceptance/Being True to the Self

Each participant at some point in the interview voiced the need for African American clergy women to live fully in who they were without attempting

---

29. See Piggue, "African American Clergy Women," 163.
30. See Piggue, "African American Clergy Women," 162.

to copy or mimic others. The conversation about authenticity would engender passionate commitment to reclaim what may have been relinquished in some ways unintended:

> Violet—"That's an interesting question you ask. A couple of things— One of the things we face is being true to who we are as women preachers and pastors. We so often try to imitate men and it just doesn't work. There is a nurturing side of God, and we should be able to live into that."[31]

> Spirit—"Resisting fitting in and getting the acceptance of black male clergy. Not perpetuating the same stuff as a clergy woman. . . . If you keep it suppressed you still can be destroyed by not doing what you are called to do. To thine own self be true."[32]

Frankie had a great deal to convey in this area as well as in the subsequent sub-headings. She shares very candidly and passionately as she engages the question of challenge faced by African American clergy women. Her responses speak deeply to her concerns, experiences, and commitment to health as a womanist embracing greater self-awareness in relation to the body and factors that play a role in our healing on various levels:

> Frankie—"Inability to be authentic, because we struggle with who we are which I feel is wrapped up in our notion of our bodies; what our bodies do; our relationship to or bodies; feelings of not being worthy; the notion that I can be a conduit—that I can serve as this sort of portal for the Divine to work through; and not only solely for black clergy women but many women globally. The other side of that is the challenge that comes with determining to be authentic which does not mesh with the portrayal of what a clergy woman is. It may block others from seeing me because it's outside of the box of those limitations. Models are few and far between, so styles are modeled after men and even leadership is shaped by hierarchical top-down reminiscent of patriarchal values. Ways we have been taught to be subservient—just to systems. We refuse to be liberated."[33]

---

31. See Piggue, "African American Clergy Women," 162.
32. See Piggue, "African American Clergy Women," 163.
33. See Piggue, "African American Clergy Women," 163.

Psychological Trauma

Frankie continues to highlight what she feels is the psychological impact on African American clergy women and the churches historical role in exacerbating harmful dysfunction. She is clear that this and more, as we will see in her other responses, may certainly contribute to body-mind trauma that eventually presents itself in unhealthy ways:

> Frankie—*"But in this particular population, African American women have been violated and so what that does to their esteem and what ways in which they have cut off parts of themselves as methods of survival. Questions of worthiness related to being called and what that means. . . . The Christian Evangelical system . . . has done well in infiltrating our psyche to make us believe that we should be disconnected from ourselves, that we should live these compartmentalized lives and that nothing good can come from this. . . . So I don't know, we just live out of 'parts' of ourselves—it almost sounds like a bi-polarity, in the sense that it's a schism that is so real. If you think about it sensibly, it doesn't even make sense."*[34]

Religious Oppression

Frankie further builds on the reality of oppressive experiences imposed by the church and the irrationality of such impositions, especially on Black people, who know what it is like to have bodies that have been subjected to violation, ownership, and degradation yet do not consider these in light of religious thought and practices that call for the body to be diminished:

> Frankie—*"The propaganda—again, the Christian Evangelical system has really done a bang up job on us, on everybody, but particularly on those bodies that have been seen in this context of the US and really globally as marginalized and contested as not human or less than."*[35]

---

34. See Piggue, "African American Clergy Women," 163–64.
35. See Piggue, "African American Clergy Women," 163.

Theological Distortions

As Frankie continued to share, she raised very intriguing insights about theological distortions related to the Incarnation. Her comment is around the notion that in light of a celebrated incarnational construct within Christian traditions, focus on the degradation and subjection of the body, which was God's offering to the world, seemed to undermine the very foundation of the religious tradition. It was a distortion that made it very difficult for her to take those who practiced such incongruence seriously. Her insight sparked my interest in revisiting the ways in which other participants had spoken about distortions, even if not explicitly. I found within a number of their responses a reflection of what Dr. Na'im Akbar calls "Unnatural Mentality,"[36] which he deems can be the root of many psychological issues. He asserts, in a similar way to what we will see Frankie question, that certain theological distortions can breed mental disturbance, as might be seen in a command to suffer as a Christian in order to obtain goodness.[37]

Frankie's focus however is very much in advocacy for the power and goodness of the body and the Black female body in particular. Historical, social, and political facets passionately accompanied her inquiry:

> Frankie—"What does it mean to tell a black person or black woman to bring your flesh under subjection? I mean what does that mean for a body that has remained under subjection since her arrival here in these United States? What does that mean to say? And what does that mean theologically to say for a group whose faith is based on this Deity incarnating this body becoming flesh? It is like a way used to police us and police our bodies, so we are just stuck trying to figure out where to be on this spectrum—can't just live in the middle because no calling would ever be fulfilled. Then of course there is the usual."[38]

In a previous question, Spirit was equally impassioned about what she felt was an absurd argument about sexuality and other mandates from religious bodies. She felt as if the arguments were inconsistent with reality and ultimately nonsensical in light of basic human behavior. Her concern was around the damage that is imposed on one's psyche and fear that controls one when attempting to live in such a bifurcated manner:

---

36. Akbar, *Community of Self*, 52.
37. Akbar, *Community of Self*, 52.
38. See Piggue, "African American Clergy Women," 163–64.

> Spirit—"*Conservative, evangelical theology renounced the body, so there was not that affirmation of the body. There was that whole Platonic split between body and spirit; the flesh is evil; you were going to hell if you engaged anything to do with the flesh. . . . So it wasn't until later in young adulthood in undergrad and grad school that you really start to ask questions about some of those things and become kind of more aware of your body and relationship with it, and start to say, 'How the hell can everything be wrong?' Why would God create people with hormones that you don't have anything to do with; you didn't choose it; it's part of your natural evolution and development and then say don't do that? Now that's ridiculous.*"[39]

I looked at several other responses within this section and found in each effects from particular ways of thinking that could easily fit under this section of theological distortion. I revisited Wanda's comment that began with the argument that no one (woman) should have to prove to anyone, simply because she is housed within a female body, that she is called to ministry. I also revisited Violet's story where she shared painfully about her father's affirmation that she was OK to preach but could not pastor because it would mean telling a man what to do. It is my assumption that this idea was drawn from Scriptures that reinforce a women's silence in the church. Jane also shared similar concerns as a woman who is part of a denomination that does not ordain women.

The challenges and acts of oppression named among participants have remained critical in the lives of African American women for generations and unfortunately have been potential conduits for unhealthy self-identity, poor self-esteem, negative health outcomes, and on occasion untimely death. In the next section we will look more closely at models and influences of early life messages and the potential impact imposed upon the mind and behaviors of African American clergy women in relation to their bodies. Identifying relational and familial frameworks and patterns passed from previous generations will help to continue uncovering insights and contributing factors that may inform correlations between those and clergy women's health.

---

39. See Piggue, "African American Clergy Women," 157.

African American Clergy Women Narrating Their Sacred Stories

Early Models, Influences, and Health Correlations Explored

What models did and do you draw from to engage pastoral ministry?

How do you feel that approach has worked for you? What impact would you say that approach had or is having on your body?

The two questions listed above provided each participant an opportunity to reflect upon the foundation on which they feel their model of engaging ministry was built. Seven of the ten participants named women as their primary models. Despite the report that very few African American clergy women held "official" roles of authority in the church, it was clear that many of those same women held "unofficial" roles of authority. These women were quite powerful and influential—not only for a person like Wanda but also in the Black church overall. During our time discussing the first question, there was a profound sense of awe and sacredness present as tears and long silence filled the space between times of offering commentary. Participants shared very reverently as they in many respects venerated their foremothers:

> Wanda—"Those senior women and my grandmothers. I could see them as ministers in another day and time most of them would be pastors/clergy women. They were so Godly, I look at their strength, integrity, just honest stuff, gentle and straight. Not a lot of education, but articulate, well-read. Some were educators. I admire the fact that I was able to compete in college because they helped to educate me and prepare me. I am still drawing on what they gave me. When I went to my first job at _____ I stood in front of women and thanked all of them."[40]

Violet had similar experiences and echoed Wanda's comment about church women who may not have been formally educated or seminary trained but had a great deal of knowledge and wisdom to offer. They were able to lead even while facing bias and the limitation of particular roles that had been assigned to them at the time. They did it while rising above the many challenges that served as obstacles in their own lives:

> Violet—"Well I didn't grow up with women as models in the church other than my Sunday school teachers (laugh). And they wore the

---

40. See Piggue, "African American Clergy Women," 164–65.

> *white training outfits, dresses and hats. So models as a pastor no. By the time I went to seminary there were a fair number of women as models and I really did have a slight problem with being a woman called into ministry myself. I think sometimes women have challenges with men thinking we are trying to take over everything. I had a few people serve as models for me in ministry. There were some very special women that I knew. One person told me when I accepted my call to ministry, 'Just be yourself, bring all that you are into ministry—Just be you.' The other thing she told me is, 'Love the people and let them love you,' and those two things have stayed with me all these years. She was probably one of my best models. She was not one of these eloquent orators; she actually had a little bit of a stutter. She didn't try to be manly in the pulpit. She was genuine and sincere and she loved the Lord and God's people."*[41]

As we continued in dialogue, the power and beauty of the participant's reflections and honor for the women who had gone before them remained empowering and deeply spiritual. It could be said that we invoked the ancestors who joined us for such a time as the one set aside to remember them in this manner:

> Frankie—*"The women I grew up with around the table having plain conversation—the vernacular, the cues, the ways of knowing through those relationships. The everyday life experiences of Black women. Gaining and sharing knowledge from the bottom up—not a top down way. Plain talk everyday way. I need not be anyone other than myself at the table—the proverbial pulpit. Love the line from For Colored Girls, 'And I loved her fiercely'!"*[42]

> Rachael—*"My mother. I did and I do because she was curious, engaging and she was accepting. She was not judgmental. She was also very open to people. She believed that everyone deserved an opportunity to live and be loved. There was a woman in my community, V, who was a Civil Rights activist and who was—kind of didn't allow others to put limits on her or tell her what to do. She was like a lawyer. In consciousness more, I think I draw on her. People who have done something and obviously has had to work to do it, is a model. Katie Canon. For the reasons that I've mentioned. You know she blazed the trails, and she persisted."*[43]

---

41. See Piggue, "African American Clergy Women," 165.
42. See Piggue, "African American Clergy Women," 166.
43. See Piggue, "African American Clergy Women," 166.

African American Clergy Women Narrating Their Sacred Stories

Of the ten participants, five included male leaders along with their significant female models who also served important roles in ministry formation. These were men who had blessed them to proceed during times when things could be very difficult for women. Participants reported that both biological and spiritual father's deposited valuable insight, affirmation, and acceptance that would help to frame their future ministry. These models also seemed to serve the role of advocate when others would attempt to limit or restrict women who had answered their call to ministry and were ready to seriously engage their journey:

> Autumn—"The first model was my own mother who is eighty-six—would have been in ministry at another time. She is very compassionate, speaks words of wisdom, is very loving and tender. Want to be more like my mother, she is very soft. The other person would be C—she had a fire when I met her. I really wanted that fire and R has the Truth—she's the biting truth teller. And actually there are some men. My pastor A, the way he walks among people and meets them where they are. It comes from my loving—I love hard. My chaplain at College—Had a justice model I grew from in terms of changing the world. I've come into my own and they have been inspiration—I am further emboldened."[44]

> Jane—"Two models out of my history—One was the strong black women that I grew up with. Women that learned to survive amidst great odds and who taught me that I could do anything. They never saw limitation. You can do anything you put your mind to, and if you believe that God has called you to do. My mom is that person. She created spaces for me to do it. I also had one pastor. In the time frame when I was moving into ministry, he was the one person who defied all the other men who said that women couldn't preach. He was the first to bring women into our congregation, and allow them to preach from the pulpit, to say I've been waiting for you to acknowledge your call and to be ordained. So that was my model. He did not let anyone define for him what he believed about God and who God called to preach. I have been fortunate to be affirmed and supported within religious traditions."[45]

> Yvette—"My mother and father who made room and made enough for others to be helped and fed in some ways. Painful experiences from my past and my opportunity to really see the Lord. I was bitter

---

44. See Piggue, "African American Clergy Women," 165.
45. See Piggue, "African American Clergy Women," 166.

and needed a lot of prayer and healing. Getting through it was a model on which I draw to do ministry. Forgiveness was necessary. There were no female pastors in my church growing up. Family systems has helped me to have a model of understanding ministry."[46]

Spirit—*"Hindsight, my great uncle—pastor of my home church, it was his humility. He had a doctorate, very conservative on some things, but approachable-had a fairly large church. . . . Believed in strong preaching, heaven or hell, but the way he dealt with people—Encouraged people to be active in ministry if you were called. Grandmother was the pastor of junior church. Accepted call later in life. Had large group of ministers in his church and strong Bible study, reading teaching Sunday school—you did it if you were called. I saw a woman pastor and felt emotional, heard my call. I had homiletical gifts. Was ordained in another denomination because my conservative one wouldn't ordain me. Wouldn't accept when I went to seminary; so worked in another denomination. It was a shared model of leadership. Wanted to embrace a model of ministry to decentralize the pastor and practice shared leadership—an empowerment model."*[47]

Lex—*"My aunt being strong and holding down everything. But I saw the other side of things eating her apart trying to be that strong woman. Seeing her be that, but at the same time watching her kill herself because she was not listening to her own body (tears). She continued to encourage me, but didn't take care of her self—would still smoke. Whatever she was dealt, she managed to handle it. Also, my mom, who by most textbooks would say she was not a good mother, but I learned what to and not to do. I don't see it as shame, I see it as she did what she had to do to get by. So for now, I can identify with some of the children I minister to and use the success of my own situation. I appreciate it now and more than willing to share. ALSO—my peers and my friends, encouraging me to go forward and not stay in one place—there is something better for you. ALSO—My pastors—I see in a different light the way that I should esteem a man and take kindness from a man. And from the woman, a harder message of 'take it, learn from it, then move from there.' No victimization."*[48]

---

46. See Piggue, "African American Clergy Women," 165. Yvette references "family systems" as a psychological concept gained in her theological education that has assisted her in understanding how to navigate painful relational dynamics.

47. See Piggue, "African American Clergy Women," 165.

48. See Piggue, "African American Clergy Women," 166.

One of the ten participants reported having no models and therefore shared the choice she felt she had to make as a result:

> Sharon—*"Because I saw so few female ministers, I had to develop my own (model). I decided that I was going to be who I was. I have seen some who are dictatorial and difficult try to be like men or protect themselves from being mistreated so they put a shell over themselves and I knew I didn't want to do that. So I made up mind to do things my way. Am I going to be bad, and tough and roll my neck or was I going to be myself because I'm not like that."*[49]

How do you feel that approach/model has worked for you? What impact would you say that approach/model had or is having on your body?

The subsequent question of the chapter builds upon revealed awareness of the impact of significant historical relationships. In this regard, taking a step further to explore how particular models have been working for the participant was an important task toward discovery of possible correlations between certain life practices and health-related outcomes. Because the question had two parts, the initial segment of answers were positive in many respects, as participants honored and appreciated the investment their mentors, models, pastors, friends, and family had contributed to their becoming/evolution in ministry. As participants discussed their experiences further (in response to the second part), they spoke with clarity and insight about growing knowledge related to these influences and the possible impact upon their bodies. During this segment, seven of the ten participants reported having experienced negative health outcomes that were of major concern in their lives at one time if not currently.

A natural response to the subsequent question, *"Have you experienced negative health outcomes since adulthood?"* began to occur almost in tandem with the question of bodily impact from using particular models. I therefore thought it appropriate to include those responses in the set of participant statements to follow.

Violet shared the following regarding the impact of early models on her life and ministry:

---

49. See Piggue, "African American Clergy Women," 166. Sharon uses slang commonly familiar to Black women "going to be bad, and roll my neck," which implies communicating with attitude, that could be off putting to one unfamiliar with the action.

> Violet—*"That approach especially worked for me—the part about bringing my full self to ministry—that affirmed that God had called me. As a person who grew up being reserved and to recognize that some good could come out of me bringing all of me into the church, and in that—the me that was called. I didn't have to try to be anybody else because it was Me that was called and that was good enough. And the other part of loving the people and letting the people love you—well sometimes it's really hard. For me to let people love me meant that I had to humble myself and let people sometimes take care of me which was not the easiest thing to do. It also meant that I had to let them serve me. I had no problem serving them. It was probably because I always felt I needed to be doing for other people. It was probably a way of being affirmed. And maybe it was my role because when young I was supposed to take care of my brothers and sisters, so you are supposed to take care of other folks instead of them taking care of you. The other part is that it's really hard for women to succeed in the church sometimes. I think because there were so many people who did not want me in as a pastor so to be able to love people who do not want you is really hard. I was mistreated in many ways. . . . So you have to learn how to move beyond your feelings to get to that place that is a step away that says I have to move beyond this in order to love the people. You have to realize that your calling is for them, not go back and forth with them, but love them. Love will take care of things eventually."*[50]

After Violet's initial comments about the way in which models have informed her practice of ministry and the impact it continues to have on her evolving thought, she turned to very significant sharing about the ways in which African American clergy women tend to overwork, overly sacrifice, and forego care of the body. It reflected many ideas shared by womanist writers, therapists, and others concerned about such imbalances too often imposed and accepted by those in leadership roles. It is akin to what Chanequa Walker-Barnes terms "No Cross, No Crown," derived from a 2004 Essence Magazine article by Renita Weems, wherein she describes large numbers of African American women who see faithfulness as self-sacrificing behavior requiring enduring suffering for the sake of "the people."[51] Walker-Barnes goes on to mention how the church can reinforce notions that Black women are expected to be strong regardless of the circumstances

---

50. See Piggue, "African American Clergy Women," 167.
51. Walker-Barnes, *Too Heavy a Yoke*, 134.

in their lives.⁵² In her quote above, Violet articulates this dynamic in her own life and cautions against early life messages that can often remain a driving force within the lives of clergy women—a caution against the expectation to care for others without regard for the self. Violet's mandate to be responsible for and to care for her siblings was still very much alive even when sacrificing for those not in that family constellation but rather in replication of her family system.

As Violet continued to share, she offered more specific thoughts about care of the body and how her thinking has altered over the years:

> Violet—"One thing that I am aware of is that ministry lends itself to workaholism, in that we don't take good care of our bodies. And I think there was probably a part that I associated loving with doing. And that meant I had to do. I was constantly available, so wasn't taking care of my body. So my body was not the first thing that came to my mind. It was having to fulfill my call to ministry and doing church work. So I think that I haven't loved my body. I should love my body which is me—as much as I do others. If I look at what I do for others that shows my love for others, and what I do for myself that shows my love for myself, I would take extremely good care of me. I would eat all the right foods, do all the exercise and pamper myself—I haven't done that. The effect that it has had on my body has been rough. It could be that some of the stress that came from ministry and taking care of others may have contributed to my cancer. I know that today I still don't take as good of care of my body as I need to and would love to. I just have discovered the joy of bed time. It came as a result of teaching Sabbath keeping. I had a group of people I was teaching to choose children's books to read and reflect upon. I did it also. So I choose one that focused on bedtime. But I discovered that I looked forward to doing things for others but also need to look forward to rest and rejuvenation. So having the ways I described of doing ministry has taken a toll on my health."⁵³

She continued in dialogue about her experience with particular negative health outcomes:

> Violet—"Yes, I do think that stress has taken its toll on me in lots of ways. When a person is in ministry, people expect that they are always available and available to them. That meant that my sleep got disturbed from time to time or I ate the wrong food because I

---

52. Walker-Barnes, *Too Heavy a Yoke*, 135.
53. See Piggue, "African American Clergy Women," 167.

didn't go home and others would feed me fattening food, so it has had some negative affect on my health. And the stress too of getting emotionally involved with people that you work with and to have them die on you or to have them turn on you. And the church's hurt is one of the worst hurts you can ever have. You just don't get hurt, you get wounded. So that causes poor care of one's body and soul as well. I also don't think we take time to do the devotionals we need."[54]

Autumn and Yvette also celebrated the positive contributions models had made in their lives. And like other participants, they were consistent in being challenged about how to successfully employ what had been gained from their models. They followed suit, commencing dialogue about the impact of their particular ministry models, certain models on their bodies, and what health outcomes resulted:

Autumn—*"I really have embodied them and can see a little bit of each of those people in me. Grateful for those wonderful relationships that have helped to make me who I am and to teach me how to love myself even when they may not have gotten it quite right. I was put on medication, a diuretic for high blood pressure—I didn't want the medication but, there were stressors here at the church. So I am paying attention to any impact on my body and choosing to do what I want (not what others expect)."*[55]

"[I have experienced] psychological & physical [Negative health outcomes]. The stress got to me once, it's why the high blood pressure came. I had trouble sleeping because I felt I needed to correct everything wrong in my life. I went through a real depression, so I decided to sit down with a counselor, needed to search out who fit for me. By that time, I was learning how to voice what I needed and talked with close friends. It has been incredibly difficult for me to find people to talk to because people are afraid and hold me in high esteem. I'm going to go get help if I need it. C is the person I can call to tell the most intimate details of my life. It was like giving it to God. Felt I've been healthy ever since."[56]

Yvette—*"It has worked in that it makes me a lot more attentive and empathetic toward the people I work with. You run across all types of family dynamics. Because I have been negligent about my self-care*

---

54. See Piggue, "African American Clergy Women," 169.
55. See Piggue, "African American Clergy Women," 168.
56. See Piggue, "African American Clergy Women," 169–70.

African American Clergy Women Narrating Their Sacred Stories

> *I tend to be full speed ahead because I'm so passionate about this pastoral care thing. I started ministry for women off the street. As a result I got really involved with friendship with these folks and in the hot seat because of what they get themselves into. It holds me down because I have not been diligent for my own care."*[57]

> *The impact on my body—"I've learned the hard way that I don't know how to sit down (and care for myself). Cancer, it's something I'm having to sit down and live with now. To be quiet and seek Him more; maybe reaching up instead of out so much."*[58]

Jane also first offers insight about the positive contributions and how her models have helped to bring strength and meaning to her ministry journey. As she shifts to address how those models have worked for her, she brings in a very important issue for many in ministry: attempting to do things alone and struggling with perfectionism that may hinder appropriate requests for support, thus increasing stress-related concerns:

> *Jane—"Strong independent self-sufficient folks. So I learned really well how to function solo and not depend on anybody. But that has also been one of my greatest limitations, because at some point in your life you can't do it all by yourself. So the message of being this lone ranger/self-sufficient person takes its toll because you spend countless hours doing things that if you could reach out and ask others for help you wouldn't have to do it. It is also a burden for me because I tend to be a perfectionist, so spend hours trying to get things just right. After I spend those hours, I still say oh I missed that, I could have done or said this better. So I have high expectations of myself which create a tremendous amount of stress; which stress we all know is dangerous and harms the body. I can't turn things off, so personal life and family life can suffer, so my body suffers, because you can't keep going. My pastor who ordained me literally died young in the pulpit. In word he said I need to figure out the balance, but he didn't. My models teach me how to be strong, self-sufficient, but not so much how to care for myself. They teach me how to give out, but not so much how to take in?"*[59]

> *Negative health outcomes?—"I've been pretty healthy most of my life. Took a turn in later years, not sure if it was stress related. Anxiety*

---

57. See Piggue, "African American Clergy Women," 168.
58. See Piggue, "African American Clergy Women," 170.
59. See Piggue, "African American Clergy Women," 168.

and depression was present, but I pushed through it in younger years. Physically, there are things that just happen related to child bearing and such. I do have a tremendous amount of stress. Blood pressure is creeping up—never had high blood pressure. If I will keep exercising and eating right I can manage it. Had surgery and hysterectomy."[60]

Both Sharon and Lex were clear that the models they were presented with early in life did not necessarily work well for them. Consequently, they spent significant time trying to figure out what they should do related to ministry. It was not until later in life that they both met models who helped them to even take a step forward in answering their call to ministry. Sharon felt that she was still working to figure it out even today and that her current illness could be an outcome of her very difficult journey:

Sharon—*"It does not work that well for me. I feel voiceless. I don't feel I carry the authority I need. I'm not aggressive enough. I can't chastise in a calm and gentle way. I'm too nice and the body could take a hit for that. But I don't know about it. Breast cancer came, then many things, but before then I didn't have any trouble before then that I may not have noticed. I didn't have all these things that are more apparent now."*[61]

Lex—*"Models definitely have impact on my body. The message of suck it up. Also internalizing things, I see it manifest in sickness in my body. So how to handle this and knowing it can be changed. Eating right, exercising—those things can be changed. Not that models were not trying—they were working with what they had."*[62]

About negative health outcomes—"I didn't realize when I had the stroke that it was related to ministry because I was bottling up things. Anything anyone wanted I did. I was not eating right, vitamins, exercise, all of that stuff. Had headache for two weeks pre-cursor to stroke, and was still trying to get to work. Three or four days were required for observation. Couldn't pin-point it—stress related. Just kept on pressing my way."[63]

Spirit and Frankie jumped immediately into dialogue about how their new models of care are working for them today. Because their early models

60. See Piggue, "African American Clergy Women," 170.
61. See Piggue, "African American Clergy Women," 168.
62. See Piggue, "African American Clergy Women," 168–69.
63. See Piggue, "African American Clergy Women," 170.

reinforced the value of their voice without limitation due to gender, age, or race, they shared more about their current experiences. Related conversation from other questions during the interview process reinforce here that they have run into challenges related to living out the positive messages from earlier in life. It seemed that once they entered ministry, on occasion they happened to experience a lack of support and/or treatment that was incongruent with the positive early messages to which they were accustomed:

> Spirit—*"Has worked in terms of self-care and is still in process. Has helped me understand the importance of rest. Pray your strength and delegate to your weaknesses. My self-care has been helpful and to be in a space where people see me struggling week to week and not have to be afraid. It's ok and not shaming. My last church struggled with seeing brokenness—embodied brokenness disturbed them. Has taught me self-care and importance of accountability partners. For Spiritual reasons—like reclaiming life-giving rituals."*[64]

> Frankie—*"The approach works wonders for me. It is liberating, it is a salvific approach meaning being liberated from the fear of death. So that would be an African centered womanist method. Liberated from the fear of death either by my own hands of killing my voice because I'm trying to dim my light so that others won't feel so intimidated by the light I come with or death because I came to the world to speak truth to power. I loved her and I loved her fiercely."*[65]

As both Spirit and Frankie considered the question of bodily impact from models and what they feel may be resulting negative health outcomes, they had this to share:

> Spirit—*"I had issues with stability, sensitivity to heat, standing, was rushed to hospital took a few years to get an actual diagnosis, ruled out many other things—invisible disability. All the mental gymnastics and having to share that in light of my vocation and public speaking. Learning how to live with it; a very rare condition. It's another thing in addition to being black and a clergy woman."*[66]

> Frankie—*"Issues with the kidney . . . and as a result of not knowing the problem, I had complications that caused other trouble; scar*

---

64. See Piggue, "African American Clergy Women," 168.
65. See Piggue, "African American Clergy Women," 168.
66. See Piggue, "African American Clergy Women," 170.

> *tissue grew as a result. Doesn't work optimally, so stabilization is the goal. Stress related factors don't help. Had a hospitalization also. Reproductively, complications with births and my body. Explored alternative medicine."*[67]

Only three of the ten participants reported having never experienced any major negative health outcomes in their life, especially as it relates to replicating early models. Wanda reports having specifically picked up a very useful practice that, in this study, might suggest key elements in deterring the impact of harmful energetic forces from finding ground within the body on which to join or take root. It is the idea, according to neuroscientist Antonio Demasio, that at the cellular level there would be no identification with a particular message and, consequently, less ability to find ground and map within the body.[68] Dr. Christiane Northrup, MD, might suggest that Wanda and her early models understood on some level that emotional and mental energy can become physical within the body.[69] Therefore, they practiced regular release of negative energy in order to allow healing to take place when racial and gender oppression threatened to be a constant assailant:

> Wanda—*"It's worked for me because the era I grew up in was oppressive, still where grandmother had to look down, say yes mam to younger white females, which took strength. It taught me to know that there are times to speak and not to speak, but for a different reason today. It was for survival then, but for not internalizing things today. I do not have to take medication because I learned certain lessons about how not to internalize."*[70]

To the question of negative health outcomes, Wanda reports that in traumatic experiences she was confronted with decisions that would affect her health negatively. However, as a general rule, she valued the practice

---

67. See Piggue, "African American Clergy Women," 170.

68. See Damasio, *Self Comes to Mind*, 68, where he speaks about the brains ability to construct maps continuously—maps that recall objects from the brains' memory bank drawn from occurrences with the body. It can include objects that sit outside the body, actions that occur outside the body, and relationships that objects assume in time and space relative to each and to the body organism.

69. See Northrup, *Women's Bodies, Women's Wisdom*, 66–67, where she discusses the significance of how thoughts and emotions affect energy within the female body; specifically, how they are reflected and/or patterned simultaneously with the brain and other organs and can manifest themselves in an individual's body.

70. See Piggue, "African American Clergy Women," 167.

of not internalizing issues that could exacerbate illness. She had this to say about her experience of negative health outcomes:

> Wanda—"Yes, periodically because I don't always get it right all the time. I used to get migraines. When first husband died and I felt stress about raising our son alone. When I let go of things, I do better. I experienced some anxiety at one point and used prayer and meditation to calm it."[71]

Rachael presented the idea of working to get things done, but with attention to taking breaks and being intentional about what one wants out of their journey. Though she was unable to find a mentor in her academic institution, she referenced the positive contributions of womanist scholars and drew strength from their work. It was clear that Rachael had strong internal resources that kept her functioning at high levels of health and invested in her well-being over the years:

> Rachael—"Persisting, I think it has worked well. That's how things get done. Keep going. Even if you have to stop and take a break, then come back, that's just how you get things done. In terms of accomplishing tasks, I would say that works. I understand the mentor as someone who kind of walks along with you. When I entered seminary and when I entered ministry, and when and where I entered, even when I entered doctoral studies, those places and spaces were filled with men who encouraged but didn't know how to take me under their wings. There was not one who—with whom I developed a relationship or who that I can say reached out to offer a relationship. In regard to the model and my body—I think the other thing about that is that I also have my own commitments to my well-being that I have crafted. So the persisting works for me and the way I have crafted how I live my life, so I persist and persisting for me includes taking care of myself. I think it should include a higher level of taking care of myself. Well I would say the two things work together. Because persisting—I want to live a long and healthy life. And I want to enjoy my older years. I have to persist in making that happen. It is part of the way I understand interacting with my body right."[72]

As an African American clergy woman myself, dialoguing with participants was quite fascinating, and because I could easily identify with experiences they shared, I was interested in and very reflective over some of the findings. Though not surprised, I came away from the interviews

71. See Piggue, "African American Clergy Women," 169.
72. See Piggue, "African American Clergy Women," 169.

deeply concerned for my particular demographic of clergy sisters. I found that Rachael is not only one of three participants (the other two are Wanda and Autumn) who reported having never suffered major negative health outcomes but also the only one of ten to have avoided even minor negative health outcomes. Her response to the question of whether she had experienced negative health outcomes took a moment for her to figure out. When she finally spoke, she commented about a slightly elevated cholesterol number:

> Rachael—*"Like high cholesterol? I'm going to take care of that. I would never have thought that I would not have managed my weight better. Because I know it has to do with what I've eaten."*[73]

Besides a desire to be a few pounds lighter in weight and engaging in preventive measures to watch her cholesterol and normal physical fitness numbers, Rachael is one of ten clergy women who has managed to keep significant balance and health in her body while carrying the weight of ministry. The distinction I found in the response that may speak to the different health outcome of Rachael is that she is one who was oriented to see her body as useful and strong early in life. She never thought herself less than her brothers but engaged in healthy competition with them. She was oriented to value her body, which at the time was useful for being fit, healthy, and strong for working the farm. So there was a mindset about the body. Conversation about sex and maturing was set within the context of nurturing your body for longevity, even though in this case it was not solely for her but for the community to benefit from her offering. Wanda has on rare occasions experienced migraine headaches and is engaging preventive measures to keep watch on her blood pressure due to heavy church demands and expectations. Autumn has situationally experienced high blood pressure and minor depression that does not persist today.

The other seven participants have experienced life-changing and physically altering illnesses that unfortunately are more common and likely among African American clergy women. It is a concern that needs more attention, investigation, and suggested means of addressing the issues at hand. As we move into the next chapter, we will continue to hear the voices of our participants and their efforts to engage healing practices in response to the final interview question. A survey of diverse healing approaches, some indigenous to one's culture, will be introduced as a way of

---

73. See Piggue, "African American Clergy Women," 170.

exploring reparative measures and ritual practices that might be employed using womanist thought and selected neuroscientific perspectives to help shape, improve, prevent, positively affect, and/or heal the revealed physical conditions African American clergy women face today.

5

Healing Approaches

To BEGIN THIS CHAPTER, I situate myself vocationally as a way of elucidating my particular lens and a great deal of what informed my interest in this topic over time. My clinical focus has been centered on facilitating the professional and personal development of clergy/spiritual leaders in ministry formation with the expressed goals of increased self-literacy and pastoral competence for ministry. Clinical Pastoral Education (CPE) engages dialogue with the behavioral sciences, yet it is not a psychotherapeutic model. Under the umbrella of Education, CPE as a national organization is accredited by the US Department of Education and adheres to standards that support the appropriate care and instruction of those who enter our programs. I therefore engaged this area of study with twenty-plus years of experience gained through CPE and the use of psychotherapeutic concepts within our educational models. Consequently, pastoral counselors and other psychotherapeutic and wellness practitioners became vital partners on this journey.

Part of my interest on this important topic originated in my work as an ACPE clinical pastoral educator with clergy/spiritual leaders who were often in my opinion asking a basic question: whether or not they had permission to think their own thoughts, take risks, and explore "forbidden" spaces within themselves without penalty. Addressing these issues of "differentiation" and "identity formation" are fairly common in these scenarios and point to early life messages and mirroring behaviors conveyed in developmental stages of life. How one responds to those messages and behaviors

Healing Approaches

are certainly influenced by multiple factors, including social, cultural, historical, personal, and communal resources that guard against imposed deterministic pathology. Theories that have informed my clinical pastoral education leadership in particular are based on relational constructs that include a communally conscious theology, a relational psychology, and andragogically-based education model.[1] I drew upon this knowledge and insight to craft the relevant interview questions for the survey instrument that was presented. In addition to my Afro-centric cultural context, it has also been a place in which I was able to nurture perspectives about community as an avenue to liberation and health. Within the CPE model, an appreciation for learning in the context of others (small groups) is thought to yield a view of oneself that is comprehensive in many ways—experiential and reflective, subjective and objective, affective, cognitive, personal, and professional.[2] It is a view that cannot be seen as easily outside such an intentionally constructed space.

My involvement and background in this work has thus allowed me the privilege of journeying with diverse people and has continued to increase my appreciation for facilitating exploration of the many faceted parts of the human person. One of those parts is the body and the ways in which we relate to her/him/them. I have discovered that the body is a part of the human person that can be easily overlooked or left out of discussions surrounding self-literacy, liberation, and, importantly, health. I do not wish to confuse the fact that conversations do occur *about* the body, but discussions seem to be fewer in number regarding one's relationship *with* one's body. This notion of a relationship with the body brought a synthesis of my interests together, holding significance for me not only vocationally and theologically but also personally. I am the women I write about, and as I continue to meet her, I continue in concern for her health and well-being, particularly while watching her, in deep dedication, ensure the care of others. While observing the imbalance of care, my question became one about the hospitality that seems to be offered easily to her community of others, but not readily to her "community of self." Too often it appears that her body is failing her, while others are being nourished by it. My understanding of a womanist approach is that it places Black women in the center as the main

---

1. See Knowles, *Adult Learner*, 32–34, in reference to his concept of "Andragogy," which he explains as regard for the wisdom and insight adult learners bring with them to the learning environment as opposed to an externally imposed pedagogy that treats the adult learner as a blank slate.

2. Hemenway, *Inside the Circle*, x.

subject of discourse, but it is also rooted in relationality that reinforces care for the survival and wholeness of all people. In an effort to define and focus this section, I draw attention to Black women as the center and main subject. This work is less about the community of others, who are inherently present nonetheless, and more about the community of self, inclusive of the body that makes her whole. What appears clearly from my research participant responses is that preferring or highly valuing the experience of Black clergy women's bodies—by others or by themselves—has not been an attended reality until unfortunately crisis transpires.

Community of the Self

Defined

"Community of the self" is that which helps to inform and frame the model of care that has been developed.[3] As mentioned in an earlier section, I restate the importance of Dr. Na'im Akbar's book, *The Community of Self,* in order to inform and emphasize the notion of a radical regard for self that is often relinquished *by* those I suggest need it most. I also emphasize the need for African American clergy women to relate and communicate authentically with all aspects of their body and mind as a unit for optimal health outcomes. They are often women who have been disembodied and out of community with the self at the hands of those who would want to gain from them without offering replenishment. Each of the ten research participants confirm that even they have on occasions embraced the destructiveness of such disembodied practices, like ignoring pain in their bodies, internalizing distorted messages of value based on sacrifice, and allowing their voice to be silenced due to historically-imposed ideology and familiar cultural norms. Contrary to what some may posit, as embraced in certain religious and cultural traditions when attention to one's own well-being is preferred, it is *not* a selfish act. It is my contention that a "community of self" that promotes self-literacy[4] and self-relationship[5] promotes wellness not only

---

3. "Community of the self" will be used interchangeably with "community of self" based on sentence structure only without intent on changing the definition offered.

4. The two together, "self" and "literacy," are my use of common terms compounded to describe the knowledge and competence one possesses about their "self" and the essential qualities distinguishing them from any other.

5. The two terms together, "self" and "relationship," are compounded to describe the way in which a person and their "self" are connected or working together and the essential qualities distinguishing them from any other.

for African American clergy women but also for the entire community. It is a womanist construct that cares not only for the self but ultimately for all who are interconnected with the one offering care. bell hooks offers a helpful way of looking at this construct through her reference of the "I" in this discourse. She affirms that it is not a signifier of one "I," but the coming together of many "I"s—the self as embodying collective reality, past and present, family, and community—it is the collective voice.[6] hooks in this discussion rejects the notion of the self existing in opposition to another that must be destroyed or annihilated, as domination or colonizing cultures attempt to do. She rather highlights what she has learned from unschooled southern Black folks about the self, existing in community wherein one's social construction in relation to community would include voices that speak in and to us from the past, calling us to be in touch with "ancient properties"—which is our history.[7]

Na'im Akbar, in his work, uses the term "community of self" to explain that one can only truly know himself/herself when they understand the parts that make up their unique self-community. He asserts that one is empowered when self-knowledge is attained—self-knowledge that comes through recognition that there are specialists within the Community of Self that perform important functions for the benefit of the whole community.[8] His composition of that community includes the following parts, each serving a particular role that if left isolated presents counterproductive activity within the self:

1. **Motors**, made of drives that are also called instincts. They serve the purpose of moving one toward pleasure or satisfaction and, in the reverse, away from pain and dissatisfaction. It is the fight or flight response. These drives are necessary, particularly for the physical survival and sustenance of a person.[9]

2. **Senses**—sight, smell, touch, hearing, and taste—are the avenues through which a person establishes contact with the outside world. They are channels through which the self receives messages and communicates. It is a base of contact and facilitates

---

6. hooks, *Talking Back*, 30–31.

7. hooks, *Talking Back*, 31.

8. See Akbar, *Community of Self*, 2–11, where he introduces the idea of specialists that perform certain functions.

9. Akbar, *Community of Self*, 2.

exchange of information within the community, yet it is only partial and incomplete.[10]

3. **Emotional ego** is the part of the community of self that speaks up for the rights of an individual to ensure that needs are not violated. It looks for support and remains sharply tuned for dangers to the self. Emotion is the tool used by the ego and responds to support and attention as well as threat and neglect. The ego has the capacity to involve and affect the entire community through emotional alarms, and if not adequately developed it can fail to support itself. Important to understand here is that in this case of failure the ego can become tyrannical and press for selfish needs.[11]

4. **Memory** serves as a type of library or archive within the community. It stores records of experiences that have gone into the building of a person. From those records, a person is guided by the light of previous lessons and rises above previous mistakes. Important with memory is that its function is as a resource and not a driver that could easily have the community locked in the past.[12]

5. **Reason**, the organizer, brings order to the information brought in by the senses. It equips the community to classify experiences in terms of time, space, quality, and other dimensions. It gives meaning and interpretation to experiences. Important to remember here is that reason judges only on the basis of facts, which can generate insensitivity to factors not always observable by reason.[13]

6. **Moral sense**, or self-accusing spirit, is the conscience that develops in order to bring justice and introduce values of good or bad, right or wrong, to the senses' observation of the environment around them. It is the moral sense that urges the self towards the development and enhancement of the highest possibilities for itself. Important here is guarding against the overly-developed conscience that demands perfection, self-sacrifice, and condemnation which can weaken the entire community.[14]

10. Akbar, *Community of Self*, 3–4.
11. Akbar, *Community of Self*, 4–5.
12. Akbar, *Community of Self*, 6.
13. Akbar, *Community of Self*, 7.
14. Akbar, *Community of Self*, 8.

7. **Willpower**, the ruler, has the unique ability to pull the mind and flesh in the direction of Truth. The will draws upon the functions of all parts of the community and unites those separate forces for the good of the whole self—community. It is the divine representative within the person, and when the will achieves ruler-ship over the self, the self grows to be the proper ruler.[15]

Akbar closes this section with an understanding that when parts of the community are properly organized and run according to their function and intended capacity, there is an inner harmony that establishes an outer community of harmony and organization for the entire world.[16]

His terminology is useful particularly because it points to a reality that we have parts of our "self" that function optimally in relationship to one another and their unique function. His emphasis on potential danger that can occur when "parts" of the community function in isolation is especially relevant to the focus on inclusion of the body's intellect and its benefit to the entire community of the self. The positive response to Dr. Akbar's work when it was first published years ago indicate that many were interested in knowing and understanding how the self is constructed in addition to having a useful concept of human development. The title of his work and selected ideas piqued my interest as well, providing a way of thinking about the parts of African American clergy women in relationship to one another and their unique function. As mentioned earlier, I was curious about the parts that often do not receive acknowledgement or even hospitality that is quickly afforded others who are not a part of her community of self. In this sense I believe hospitality includes being generous, kind, and attentive to the needs of those invited into her intimate space. For our topic, that would mean an invitation to the parts of herself that have never been invited.

I elected to shift the focus of Akbar's community of self from the psychological components of the mind to a focus on the physical body within the community of the self in dialogue with the mind and spirit. Such focus recognized and supported some of the insights I grew to understand within the field of neuroscience; insights suggesting that dialogical energy exchange between parts of the body occur at all times and through which I propose is a means of employing healing practices.

---

15. Akbar, *Community of Self*, 9–10.
16. Akbar, *Community of Self*, 10.

I suggest that a "re-valuing" of the body as part of the community of self be used as a way to introduce one to self-relationship that significantly includes the body. In addition, the same process of re-valuing can be used to contest historically disempowering messages that have contributed to the dis-embodiment of Black women, who indeed see and use their bodies but, as noted in many of the participant responses, were never formally introduced to her. Consequently, I submit that a lack of introduction and absence of intentional valuin, gives her and others more access to use, misuse, and devalue what is one of the most powerful and amazing life forces to ever exist—the Black female body fully invested within her community of self.

A Pastoral Psychological Framework Design: Toward a Constructive Embodied Framework for Preferring and Addressing the Care of African American Clergy Women's Bodies

Eight questions were asked during my qualitative interviews. From participant responses the question of whether African American clergy women have viewed their physical bodies equally as valuable as the more intangible parts of themselves was evidenced. Nine reported that they had never been formally introduced to their body and consequently had not valued, known, or even considered the concept of a relationship with their body until possibly later in life or when illness struck. From these findings, I concluded that an appropriate first step toward a constructive, embodied framework that promotes a re-valuing of the body was through formal introduction. I suggest that an introductory ritual, despite whether one feels they have a current sense of body awareness, be engaged through use of the first two questions of the research survey tool: "What were the early messages received about your body?" and "How would you describe your relationship with your body—in youth, young adulthood, and currently?"

When these questions were engaged in the interview setting, there was to some degree unexpected yet remarkably powerful and intimate sharing by research participants. I believe this occurred in part because their stories were being taken seriously, and many reported having never sat with the particularity of what they considered very important questions. The distinction for them was that the questions were not "about" their body but about their relationship "with" their body. As a result, the conversation evoked deep emotion (pain and pleasure) and placed them front and center without interruption or interpretation from the interviewer. The other factor I believe informed such powerful sharing was the provision of a safe and welcoming space, not defined in the physicality of location alone but the hospitable energetic[17] space that conveyed expansive capacity to hold their story and whatever accompanied it.

Restated, I subscribe to a relational psychology, one of which heavily informs my work with groups and individuals in the creation of such spaces. A theory to which I subscribe is Donald Winnicott's concept of the "facilitating environment," where exploration and risk can be engaged and held by one or others who serve the role of "good enough mothering."[18] "Mothering" in this capacity does not hold gender specificity. In this sense, if an environment is safe, adaptable, and good enough, it can facilitate the process of maturation, as opposed to an unsafe environment that can potentially lead to isolation, compliance, and ultimately the creation of a false self.[19] Also important in this object relations theory is the idea of "integration" and "holding" during the maturational process (developmental stages).

Affirming the body as a vital part of the community of self reflects in some ways the importance of attending to stages in the maturational process. For example, the lack of introduction to the body quite possibly sets the stage for neglect of very crucial identity formation and subsequently stages on which that task is built. Stages in Winnicott's maturational process include integration, personification, and object relating.[20] Michael St. Clair offers brief definitions for each of these stages in *Object Relations and Self-Psychology: An Introduction*:

> *Integration* suggests the increased organization of the individual into a unit, since the personality does not begin as a completed whole. *Personification* refers to the way in which the individual's psyche becomes localized in the body. *Object relating*, for Winnicott, has to do with feeling real and relating to real people and actual objects in the environment; this differs, of course from the usual meaning of object relations as an inner process.[21]

17. I use this language as a way of describing the energy field between me and the participant that had been prepared intentionally in an effort to support her sacred offering without judgement or limitation.

18. Winnicott, *Maturational Processes and the Facilitating Environment*, 65–67.

19. Winnicott et al., *Home Is Where We Start From*, 33.

20. Winnicott et al., *Home Is Where We Start From*, 28–32.

21. See Clair, *Object Relations and Self Psychology*, 69, where he discusses Donald

Our Bodies Are Alive

The components of this strain of object relations theory compliment the goal of integrating the body into the whole unit of the community of self. Personification corresponds to the idea of the body-mind connection localized within the community of self and points to the argument that the body holds maps and encoding of one's experiences, good or bad. In the context of developing a constructive framework for healing African American clergy women's body-relationships, successful object relating speaks to the notion of feeling real and relating to real people or actual objects in the environment. In this case, the real object becomes the neglected body that has not been considered an equal and vital part of the whole.

Given the significance of this foundational work, it is important to seriously consider how intentional space is created for the re-valuing of the body that may be introduced to the community of self for the first time. Therefore, as a model was developed, first steps included creating, preparing and entering spaces reverently in order to facilitate and hold what would be engaged in healing work, such as healing dialogue, healing acts, reflection, grief, and celebration. This process would entail a revisiting of incomplete developmental tasks that were quite possibly "skipped over" yet are very crucial to early identity formation of African American clergy women, related to intimate knowledge and conception about their body.

Two popular literary productions helped to inform my vision for crafting a womanist constructive embodied framework for preferring and addressing the care of African American Clergy women's bodies: Toni Morrison's *Beloved* and Ntozake Shange's *For Colored Girls Who Have Considered Suicide/When the Rainbow Is Enuf*. These two pieces of literature hold at the center of their messages a core element for embodied healing—The necessity of *LOVE* for the body and recognition that loving in this manner is a spiritual practice that leads to greater wholeness.

The first is the well-known, very stirring prophetic sermon held in the woods by Baby Suggs in Toni Morrison's *Beloved*. It is a poignant illustration of calling Black people to attention about the need to *Love* their bodies in very tangible and intentional ways—by seeing, touching, nurturing, and celebrating its beauty and value when others would treat it otherwise:

> Here, she said, "In this place, we flesh; flesh that weeps, laughs; flesh that dance on bare feet in grass. Love it. Love it hard. Yonder they do not love your flesh. They despise it. They don't love your eyes; they'd just as soon pick 'em out. No more do they love the skin on our back.

Winnicott's stages in the maturational process in brief.

Healing Approaches

> Yonder they flay it. And O, my people, they do not love your hands. Those they only use, tie, bind, chop off and leave empty. Love your hands! Love them. Raise them up and kiss them. Touch others with them, pat them together, stroke them on your face, because they don't love that either. You got to love it, you! This is flesh I'm talking about here. Flesh that needs to be loved.... So love your neck... and all your inside parts.... The dark, dark liver—love it, love it and the beat and beating heart, love that too. More than eyes or feet. More than lungs that yet have to draw free air. More than your life-holding womb and your life-giving private parts, hear me now, love your heart. For this is the prize."[22]

We hear in Baby Suggs words a challenge against accepting the fallout of self-hatred and degradation of the body produced by inhumane acts of slavery, lynching, and other racially motivated acts of violence. I've addressed the fact that African American women have been significantly alienated from their bodies due to influences rooted in painful history—a history wherein Black bodies were commodified and owned by white Americans who chose to define Black bodies for their own purposes. Baby Suggs in this passage brings an alternative to the legacy of imposed self-hatred. She proclaims hope in a choice to love Black bodies that can instead of being hated, become sites for healing and loving fiercely. Yet, from research participant responses, like Violet's statement:

> "So for about ten years I should have been proud of my body, because it was probably the time in my life when it was close to perfect, but it had been such a difficult time growing up that I hadn't gotten to the point of being able to appreciate my body until the illness showed up. And that just messed it up."[23]

Or like Sharon's lament, it appears that a regard for the beauty, specialness, and importance of the body has not translated well over time.

> "As an older person my relationship is one of disgust. Not because it's not attractive but my interest is more about my health and how I feel rather than what it looks like; and I haven't felt well in my body. I wish I had appreciated the health that I had because I was very healthy as a young adult. I was a runner and was strong, had excellent memory, my mind was good. I'm seeing myself on the decline as

---

22. Morrison, *Beloved*, 92–94.
23. See Piggue, "African American Clergy Women," 155.

an older person and I am not happy about that at all. So it's a source of aggravation. It hurts."[24]

Despite amazing accomplishments and more favorable experiences with the body today, there is much work to be done toward a loving and embodied way of relating to the "self."

The other literary work is Ntozake Shange's *For Colored Girls Who Have Considered Suicide/When the Rainbow Is Enuf.* Shange presents very powerful monologues that capture the sundry and varied experiences of Black women. One line of her monologues that heralds a theologically sound position, and in many respects establishes self-love as foundational to a woman's well-being, is integral to the design of this constructive embodied framework. She illustrates poetically the goal of what my hope entails for African American clergy women who look to embrace a guide for care of their bodies while continuing to engage pastoral ministry:

i found god in myself / & i loved her / i loved her fiercely.[25]

The significance of internalized value is one of a serious nature and is the focus of a considerable portion of this book Within the introduction, I state that imaging (of oneself) plays a crucial role, not only as a function of intra-psychic developmental processes informed by social and cultural factors but also as foundational to one's identity formation in terms of spirituality, self-worth, and physical health. Consequently, the ability to find God within the "self" has major implications for how one may view or accept themselves and the divinity that exists within. In the Christian tradition, Scriptures like Genesis 1:26 affirm that as a creation one is loved and reflects the Imago Dei: "Then God said, let us make humankind in our image, according to our likeness."

An understanding of this notion comes through early and subsequent experiences of object relating that helps one mirror the part of them that is in need of integration and personification related to a God consciousness.[26] Of course, early maturational processes are not the only challenges to one's ability to find God as part of the self. In orthodox religion, for women who have been identified as the gender "other than God's," it has at times been challenging to mirror what has not been reflected as a result of sexism. Within Christianity and society in general, the message of loving the

---

24. See Piggue, "African American Clergy Women," 158.
25. Shange, *For Colored Girls*, 63.
26. Winnicott et al., *Home Is Where We Start From*, 33.

self and seeing God within, especially for Black people, has been a major obstacle for other reasons according to Riggins Earl, a professor of ethics at the Interdenominational Theological Center. In *Loving the Body: Black Religious Studies and the Erotic*, he asserts that the way in which Blacks love themselves necessitates an understanding of the pathological history of American religion and racism.[27] Because white Christianity's creation of a white soul/Black body salvation dilemma required that Blacks hate their bodies, it was difficult for Blacks to love their bodies in an anti-Black society as creations of God.[28] He goes on to stress that a redemptive God-consciousness can include one in which a person comes to image themselves in God's likeness, thus increasing their worth and ability to relate to the Divine who is like them.[29] In *Self, Culture and Others in Womanist Theology*, Phillis Sheppard speaks not only to the same dilemma raised by Riggins Earl but also to contemporary issues Black women continue to face in liberation and feminist works that left women of color on the periphery in their discourse.[30] Consequently, she commits to highlighting issues of embodiment for Black women as integral to how Black women understand themselves in the contexts in which they live and ultimately how they relate to and image God within and without. It is what I contend occurs within the line in Ntozake Shange's poem and the discovery of a god within. To find the image of a female God within and, consequently, a love that incites fierce maintenance of that divine essence is healing at its best.

Both of these works convey the goal and staple of what has to be foundational within a community of self, especially for those called to the ministry of care for others.

In the next section I highlight the select neuroscientific perspectives and somatic psychology that helped to inform examination of further data and ultimately the process of crafting a model for loving the self "fiercely."

---

27. See Hopkins and Pinn, *Loving the Body*, 267, where Dr. Riggins Earl speaks on the topic of "Loving Our Black Bodies as God's Luminously Dark Temples: The Quest for Black Restoration." The idea that a Black person could love their bodies has been an exercise in redemptive God-consciousness on the backdrop of white Christianity's insistence upon superiority and equality related to God images. Black bodies had been declared irredeemable if not washed in the blood of Jesus in order to obtain a white soul.

28. Hopkins and Pinn, *Loving the Body*, 250.

29. Hopkins and Pinn, *Loving the Body*, 264.

30. Sheppard, *Self, Culture, and Others*, 14.

6

What Select Neuroscientific Perspectives and Somatic Psychology Offer a Conversation on Healing Practice

NEUROSCIENCE OFFERS VERY INTERESTING and exciting ways of exploring some of the challenges many have faced over time related to embodiment, particularly African American clergy women and the imposed demands of living in a disembodied manner that continues to serve the needs of others primarily at the expense of her own health and well-being. Somatic psychology offers similar insights using a familiar lens and clinical language to address this dynamic.

I highlight selected points that are deemed relevant to a basic understanding of neuroscience and how it speaks to the health outcomes of African American clergy women and the issue of internalized messages. The first term is referred to as "body mapping." In this regard, I found neuroscientist Antonio Demasio's writings about the body-brain, body-mind conception helpful. In light of the topic surrounding African American clergy women and disembodiment, an explanation of how the brain maps significant events and stores them within the body was most useful. The other informative concept has to do with an understanding that communication occurs at all times between the body and brain, and that only the body can substantiate that the communication is occurring.

What Select Neuroscientific Perspectives and Somatic Psychology

Demasio explains that neurons share most of the characteristics of other cells in the body yet have a distinctive operation. Neurons can send signals not only to other neurons but also to other cells within the body; therefore, neurons exist for the benefit of all other cells.[1] They assist by receiving signals and either promoting the release of chemical molecules or by making movements happen. They eventually come to mimic the structure of parts of the body to which they belong and end up representing the state of the body by literally mapping the part for which they work, like a neural double.[2] Mapping, he continues, is the brain's way of informing itself. They create images which are the main currency of the mind. Maps are constructed when we interact with objects, be it a person, machine, place, from outside of the brain toward its interior. They are also constructed when we recall objects in our sleep. The human brain maps whatever object sits outside it, whatever action occurs outside it, and all the relationships that objects and actions assume in time and space relative to each other and the body. It has the ability to represent aspects of the structure of non-brain things and events as well, which includes the actions carried out by our body's components.[3] Two other important points are that by mapping its body in an integrated manner, the brain manages to create the critical component of what will become the self. Demasio also notes that the body does not operate as a single unit but rather has components that remain in constant dialogue.

The following holds significant implications for this topic about nurturing intentional relationship with the body given that the self is informed through integration of body-mind function and ongoing communication that can understandably inform health outcomes. If, like many of the research participants, a formal introduction and valuing of the body was limited to non-existent, then mapping occurrences could potentially preclude positive imaging, messages, or energy within the body related to body conception. In such a case, it would rather have scripted the negative messages nine of ten participants reported were their common experience. If a message of being too dark, skinny, or ugly overshadowed more nurturing exchange of care and love for the body, then subsequent messages of devaluation might be more readily received within the body as a result of familiarity with that particular type of communication. These

1. Damasio, *Self Comes to Mind*, 18–19.
2. Damasio, *Self Comes to Mind*, 41.
3. Damasio, *Self Comes to Mind*, 69.

messages could potentially lodge within the body and become a part of cellular history that reinforce similar communication and experiences. Unless new information, new energy, and intentional healing work was embraced as a means of dislodging what was familiar and harmful in exchange for positive mapping and infiltration of cellular memory, then the body could potentially hold negative cellular responses that equate to negative health outcomes. The following statement by Demasio helps us to recognize the importance of the body's ability to communicate, manage, and inform what occurs and is created within the community of self:

> Body-brain communication goes both ways, from body to brain and in reverse. The two ways of communication, however are hardly symmetrical. The body to brain signals, neural and chemical, permit the brain to create and maintain a multimedia documentary on the body, and allow the body to alert the brain to important changes occurring in its structure and state. . . . The brain knows what the past state of the body has been and can be told of modifications occurring in that state. The latter is essential if the brain is to produce corrective responses to changes that threaten life. The brain-to-body signals on the other hand, neural as well as chemical, consists of commands to change the body. The body tells the brain: this is how I am built and this is how you should see me now. The brain tells the body what to do to maintain its even keel. Whenever it is called for, it also tells the body how to construct an emotional state.[4]

In light of this analysis, I maintain my comment on the importance of recognizing the body as an integral part of the community of self and the meaning making that occurs within the dialogue between the body-mind. Attention to the body cannot merely be an afterthought, as it has been in so many cases of clergy burnout and imbalance of care often leading to illness. I raise two points here:

(1) Given the brain-body integration and its ability to map significant experiences outside, around, and within for storage, it would be an important step for African American clergy women to assess not only the familiar messages and experiences she is aware her body holds but also those to which she has not given much thought. For instance, associations she engages, be they people, places, causes, etc., would become subject to a type of deeper investigation in order to identify potential harmful messages and energy existent within those associations. In simpler terms, the

---

4. Damasio, *Self Comes to Mind*, 98–101.

What Select Neuroscientific Perspectives and Somatic Psychology

goal would be to identify particular likenesses in those with whom one spends time that may reinforce familiar messages and patterns because that person carries the same messages or patterns. It is not unlike warnings offered through parents or close relatives early in life about mindfulness related to the company one keeps. In this sense, our family member may have understood much more than the surface implications of that caution. Therefore, the construction of a womanist framework for embodied thought that prefers and addresses the care of African American women's bodies in community with the self is a necessity in the process of revaluing and engaging the healing she deserves.

(2) Given the body-brain integration and mapping realities, it appears that the practice of healing "ritual" cannot be seen or considered a simple formality but rather a transformational act. In light of these neuroscientific claims, it is my stance that healing rituals should be taken more seriously as a way of offering the body-brain an opportunity to record or map life-giving experiences from which to draw when healing is needed. A more extensive look at the importance of ritual in light of these facts will be addressed in the section on diverse healing practices. However, it is important to state here that ritual practices serve an important connection to the realm of spirit which cannot be explained scientifically, but that is an essential part of transforming acts of healing. The dialogue between body-brain inherently involves spirit as a part of the community of self and has implications for a holistic model of care that privileges all parts of the body.

Dr. Christiane Northrup, MD, author of the book *Women's Bodies, Women's Wisdom*, offers further insight on neurotransmission within the body. Her work in the medical sciences speaks significantly to common experiences women face not only related to the female anatomy but also to energy fields and systems, embodied thought, emotional cleansing, and body intelligence. She reinforces what has already been shared in this section—body organs communicate directly between the brain and vice-versa through chemical messengers she refers to as neuropeptides, a medical term for small, protein-like molecules used by neurons to communicate to one another. These chemicals, she asserts, are triggered by thoughts and emotions and are part of the way in which our feelings directly affect our physical bodies.[5] She goes on to share that our thoughts, emotions, and brains communicate directly with our immune, nervous, and endocrine

---

5. Northrup, *Women's Bodies, Women's Wisdom*, 31.

systems, and though they have been conventionally studied and viewed as separate, they are in fact aspects of the same system.[6]

Northrup's medical expertise and her inclusion of a holistic approach to medically treating patients are of importance to this study. She encourages us to expand our concept of the "mind" in that it should not be confined to the brain cavity or even intellect. She suggests that the mind exists in every cell of our bodies, and every thought we think and emotion we feel has a biochemical equivalent. A colleague in dialogue about this notion communicated the same sentiment in this way, "The mind is the space between the cells, so when the part of your mind that is . . . (a particular organ or location) talks to you, through pain . . . (or a noted reaction), are you prepared to listen to it?"[7] The critical nature of the body-mind relationship and the potential impact it has on health outcomes continues to be illustrated here.

Somatic psychology like neuroscience addresses the experience of encoding within the body. Somatic psychology works to treat the impulses of physicality, related to this encoding, as a lived experience of embodiment, thus considers it a voice that can bring awareness to holistic discourse.[8] In traditional psychodynamic theory, somatization described a process by which psychological conflict was transformed into bodily distress and could therefore describe a pattern of symptom manifestation in which emotional distress and social problems are channeled either partially or exclusively into physical ailments.[9] These definitions characterize experiences that, according to my research data, are common to African American clergy women and the challenges of being Black, female, and in ministry.

Barnaby Barratt asserts in *The Emergence of Somatic Psychology and BodyMind Therapy* that a different way of respecting our body knowledge and tailoring our behaviors accordingly is through "listening to the voice of our embodied experience," which he considers a subversive act. It is political.[10] He goes on to stress that "this listening is the refusal to treat the body as a conceptual object or thing afforded it by western culture throughout

---

6. Northrup, *Women's Bodies, Women's Wisdom*, 32.

7. Northrup, *Women's Bodies, Women's Wisdom*, 32.

8. Barratt, *Emergence of Somatic Psychology*, 46.

9. See Walker-Barnes, *Too Heavy a Yoke*, 6–7, where she references Kirmayer and Young in "Culture and Somatization."

10. Barratt, *Emergence of Somatic Psychology*, 175.

the modern era."[11] Rather, the body becomes a dialogical partner in the processes that constitute our being-in-the-world.[12] Reinforced here, the act of listening to the voice of our embodied experience can overcome what Barratt calls alienation or what I call disembodiment—experiences that have been established in the course of our socialization and acculturation. Most importantly, as we move toward a constructed model for healing, Barratt offers a useful thought:

> Our act of releasing ourselves from an alienated relation with our own embodiment is not only a procedure with social and cultural implications; it is also a restorative spiritual event. It is a revitalizing process of reconnection with the life force within us, and in this sense it is holy.[13]

In keeping with the importance of ritual as healing acts, Barrett's emphasis on spirituality as a part of bringing cohesion within the community of self and into dialogue that is always occurring is an effort toward greater wholeness. In addition, what he outlines matches the goals laid out in the healing model to follow.

Diverse Healing Practices

As previously discussed, western culture has continued to impose hegemonic notions of a dualistic and reductive program of science that unfortunately reinforces a splitting of the mind and body. It is one of the primary reasons that the type of problem addressed in this book is related to disembodiment. By contrast, there are other philosophies and practices that offer a more holistic view of the body and of the universe and focuses more on health and spiritual growth as a process of cultivating awareness. Barnaby offers the belief that cultivating awareness is a "holistic reawakening of the senses, as well as a confrontation with whatever obstructs the free-flow of spiritual and emotional energies within the body."[14]

With this in mind, the findings from research participants and an examination of diverse healing practices help to illuminate that one size does not fit all when it comes to what is meaningful, holy, and sacred to person's

---

11. Barratt, *Emergence of Somatic Psychology*, 175.
12. Barratt, *Emergence of Somatic Psychology*, 175.
13. Barratt, *Emergence of Somatic Psychology*, 175.
14. Barratt, *Emergence of Somatic Psychology*, 105.

seeking healing. Within a myriad of religions and indigenous traditions are spiritual practices tailored to address particular maladies or desires for greater awareness, prosperity, fertility, and other interests. In reflection over responses from research participants, an exploration of diverse healing practices drawn from indigenous healing traditions proved relevant.

During this time of dialogue with participants, it was heartening to witness the level of commitment most had begun to make to themselves while at the same time lamenting some of the time they felt they had lost caring for so many others at the expense of themselves. Violet made the statement that "had she cared for herself the way she cared for the folks she ministered to, she would have probably been much better off today." The idea of loving your neighbor as yourself (Mark 12:30–31) has so often been reversed in action. Interestingly enough, with our conversation about the body-mind, the earlier portion of this Scripture has even further implications for attending to the body-self for optimal mind-body-spirit existence: "Love the Lord your God with all your heart, and with all your soul, and with all your *mind*, and with all your strength." It is a command inclusive of loving the body and even further, loving in a fierce way the god within the "self."

Healing Rituals Engaged

The last interview question asked the following:

Are there rituals you engage as part of your healing practice?

In each participant's answer, it was clear that all were conscious of the necessity to engage their health differently if life and maintenance of effective ministry was to occur. Responses highlighted rituals each participant consciously had begun to practice as a means of caring for themselves. I was encouraged and hopeful for African American clergy women. As our time began to conclude, some shared that they were working to be as well as they could and also were loving their bodies in ways they perhaps never had. The question again raised significant curiosity, some disbelief, some sadness about realizations possibly missed, and motivation to become much more informed in the future.

In summary of the responses to follow, I was pleasantly surprised at the array of answers shared by participants. They included at least forty different practices that I will list here. Of the forty, three of the practices were shared by roughly half of the participants to include prayer, exercise, and music. The range certainly represented the varied ways that healing practices speak to diverse people and reinforce the idea that one size really does not fit all!

Practices included: healing touch, reading, taking walks, using home remedies, listening to a favorite theologian, acupuncture, being in community, reciting liberty confessions, Bible study, ancestral veneration, engaging body permissions and healing, saying no, regular doctor's visits, alternative energy work, rituals, affirmations, not pushing the body too much, gardening, playing indigenous instruments, feeling OK to be with self, confident to share with others, releasing things quickly, facials, bubble baths, using natural products and pampering, piddling (doing nothing), getting hair done, having scalp massage, exercising, practicing gratitude, stretching the body, yoga, going to the ocean, being in nature, placing self around beautiful things, Scripture, listening to beautiful music, prayer, massages, being anointed by someone trusted, and meditation.

It appeared that diverse healing practices spoke expressly to what was meaningful to each participant, their tradition, culture, and personality. *Integrating Traditional Healing Practices into Counseling and Psychotherapy*, edited by Roy Moodley and William West, has been a rich resource pertaining to indigenous spiritual practices from across the globe.[15] In particular, it helped offer insight about some of the practices research participants voiced. Moodley and West assert that many healing methods appear reformulated and reconstituted in the West and have been used in some ways to address shortcomings of conventional medicine and health care.[16] With this reformulation, we find people combining traditional and conventional methods for healing. It is what I gathered from our participants as they lifted the practices of acupuncture, meditation, playing indigenous instruments, and yoga as choices for facilitating healing. Anne Soloman and Njoki Wayne in this text go on to report that certain practices derive from embodied knowledge of ancestors meant to be shared with future generations. They state that "Memory is recorded literally in the viscera, in the flesh."[17] This in

15. Moodley and West, *Integrating Traditional Healing Practices*.
16. Moodley and West, *Integrating Traditional Healing Practices*, xv.
17. Moodley and West, *Integrating Traditional Healing Practices*, 55. See Solomon and Posluns, *Songs for the People*; Wane, "Learning Toward an Ecological Consciousness." As cited in chapter 5, "Indigenous Healers and Healing in a Modern World," where indigenous knowledge and how the body holds memory and "knowing" from sacred teachings and the foundations of culture is highlighted.

many ways supports the notion of body mapping that images experiences within the body.

It is my belief that some of the practices shared by research participants are also those descended from ancestral relationships that the body may know but of which the brain is unaware. I use this text to help identify particular practices that illustrate similarities to some of those shared by research participants. Please note that there was no concrete data obtained from participant narratives, neither was there extensive dialogue in relation to a particular tradition. My effort was to help identify indigenous forms of healing practice that were similar to responses offered by participants which reveal an array of options for healing work. Each participant would have to affirm direct connection to a particular tradition.

That being shared, an example, for instance, of a Zulu traditional healer who was interviewed by Soloman and Wayne, explained that one prescription of a healer is a spiritual bath, which is a formal acknowledgment that something needs to be done about physical, mental, or emotional well-being. In this act, there is submission to the water and candles as a beginning act of submission for help for oneself. The type of bath taken depends on the type of healing needed and could include salts, floral herbs, gems stones, spices, and nature items, such as rocks, pebbles, sands, or leaves, all of which depend on the healing needed.[18] This healing practice is akin to two participant responses that included taking baths, using candles, natural products, and aroma spices and herbs:

> Autumn—"I have certain natural products I use, I cleanse my face taking care to do it, don't wear any make-up some days to give it a chance to breath. Every morning I take a bubble bath and moisturize from head to toe—it is a part of my self-care because I feel different when I take care. I also have to look at my body when I do this."

> Rachael—"Yes, but they are irregular. I take baths with candles. I use a lot of lavender. I spray my bed sheets with lavender. Actually, that I do almost every time I change the bed. I use lavender soap. I take baths with Epsom soap and use lavender bubble bath—the lavender thing. . . . [When younger] we used to use Sassafras, Life Everlasting tea, even Pine tea. Though we were cautioned about those who practiced using roots."[19]

---

18. Moodley and West, *Integrating Traditional Healing Practices*, 58.
19. Piggue, "African American Clergy Women," 171–72.

What Select Neuroscientific Perspectives and Somatic Psychology

This same Zulu healer mentioned that her grandmother, who passed the gift of healing to her, practiced healing people through the medium of touch. One research participant affirmed that healing for her could come through healing touch from someone she trusts.

Wanda—*"Being anointed by someone I trust. Massages."*[20]

From Caribbean parts of the country, relying on the capacity of the body to heal itself came from the unfortunate experience of slaves who had little help for care of the body. Use of herbs, plants, ginger, and roots to address both internal and external illness was a common prescription for healing. In addition, prayers that accompanied other religious practices that became fused in the islands following Caribbean emancipation was used. Similarities to research participant responses include prayer, use of home remedies, and being in community, which was the foundation upon which emancipation from not only colonization but from many illnesses and diseases Caribbean's experienced in their uncertain and tortuous health environment.[21]

Jane—*"Seldom take medication, I avoid them. I use home remedies that are being regarded again today."*[22]

In traditional Chinese medicine, a balancing of the yin and yang forces are highly observed. A stagnation of the *qi* and blood in various body organs or both is the focus of relief and/or healing. One treatment modality matches what some of our participants use in their healing practices, and that is acupuncture. Acupuncture stimulates the flow of *qi* and removes stagnation of blood, allowing stimulation of the flow, which leads to transmission of healing energies. It is considered an alternative healing practice also mentioned among participants.[23]

Jane—*"Acupuncturist. These are all healing practices for me."*

Frankie—*"Alternative energy work. Rituals."*[24]

The Hindu practices of yoga, observing the law of karma, and consulting gurus, priests, or healers for guidance, which can include healing

20. Piggue, "African American Clergy Women," 170.
21. Moodley and West, *Integrating Traditional Healing Practices*, 74–75.
22. See Piggue, "African American Clergy Women," 171.
23. Moodley and West, *Integrating Traditional Healing Practices*, 106.
24. See Piggue, "African American Clergy Women," 171.

ceremonies and rituals, pilgrimages, prayers, and fasts, are also practices that place seekers on a quest or desire for attaining higher states of consciousness.[25] Stretching the body, yoga, practicing gratitude, and feeling confident to be with oneself were practices expressed by participants who seemed to draw from these for their well-being.

> Violet—"*I also do mediation with Oprah and Deepak Chopra which I like.*"

> Spirit—"*I alter schedule for self-care and health. Saying 'no.' If something is not working for me, getting out of it more quickly. Not holding on to what is not life-giving to me. Sitting down, not pushing my body too much, figuratively and literally.*"[26]

In Islamic tradition, healers use both medicinal remedies and spiritual means that utilize one's latent energy and power contained in devotions, supplications, and mediations of the prophets, messengers, and wise men of God.[27] Not unlike the Christian tradition, prayer, Scripture, Bible study, and listening to a favorite theologian (as noted by participants) are attempts to draw near to God in a more personal relationship. In Islam, however, there is a dedication to the specific practice of *salah* which combines body movements, recitation, Quranic verses, and supplication five times a day in addition to purification and body washing if possible.[28] The healing of ritual acts and affirmations are illustrated in this tradition in ways not required of Christianity but practiced in other ways. Several participants named a combination of similar healing practices:

> Wanda—"*Prayer is huge for me—embodied practice—having a mindset of prayer and try to live in a state of prayer at all times. Scripture reading, singing, beautiful music is comforting.*"

> Jane—"*Read, music quiets spirit decreases stress—whatever speaks to me, community is important, friends, family, the Bible is important to read—particular texts speak to me, listen to favorite theologian.*"[29]

---

25. Moodley and West, *Integrating Traditional Healing Practices*, 144.
26. See Piggue, "African American Clergy Women," 171.
27. Moodley and West, *Integrating Traditional Healing Practices*, 159–60.
28. Moodley and West, *Integrating Traditional Healing Practices*, 163.
29. See Piggue, "African American Clergy Women," 170–71.

What Select Neuroscientific Perspectives and Somatic Psychology

Buddhist meditation is a popular practice mentioned by several participants. It focuses on acquisition of self-knowledge and is carried out in non-judgmental ways. It is a process of noticing and mindful awareness. Components include flexibility of self, openness in the present moment, compassion, interconnectedness, and sitting with suffering to ultimately attain a greater state of wellness.[30] A number of participants shared the benefit of similar practices:

> Wanda—"*I love. Meditation. Exercising, gratitude confessions. Stretching body and thanks.*"
>
> Spirit—"*Being OK with being with myself in all manners. Buddhist practice.*"
>
> Autumn—"*I no longer hold onto things and if I need to say something, I take time to call right then and get it out of me. Having a trusted confidant that I can share intimately with.*"[31]

I will share more related to mindfulness meditation and its benefit for African American clergy women in the next section. Before leaving this section, however, I focus on several more traditional healing practices.

In an African-centered context, the observance of Maat contains practices that are core and resonate with our research participants as many of them are of African descent. In particular the practice of affirmations, liberty confessions, and being in community with others resonate with the practices and goals of Maat in that it seeks to help Black communities cope and manage with stressful circumstances as well as offering new pathways toward healing individuals and promoting community well-being. The practices are carried out through religious healing (music, drumming), meditation, homeopathy, spiritual healing and mentorship, self-knowledge, and the power of energy, spirit, and life forces toward holistic ways of living and relating.[32]

> Frankie—""*Alternative, energy work, rituals, foot cleansing, affirmations, body permission and healing, prayer, ancestral veneration, libation, healing touch, building esteem and reciting liberating confessions with family and children.*"

---

30. Moodley and West, *Integrating Traditional Healing Practices*, 186–91.
31. See Piggue, "African American Clergy Women," 170–71.
32. Moodley and West, *Integrating Traditional Healing Practices*, 210–18.

Our Bodies Are Alive

> Spirit—"*Spirit. Relationship between sound and healing—no words . . . healing brain through world music. Personal—Music, drumming.*"[33]

In Aboriginal healing, spirituality is central. Nature is seen as providing a sort of blueprint of how to live a healthy life. For them, a spiritual connection exists between nature and humans that is ultimately seen as part of nature. Connection with nature is then an act of getting back to creation and the Creator. Consequently, when research participants state that the ocean and water is healing, taking walks, gardening, and surrounding themselves with beautiful things, they are living examples of how the Aboriginal view the benefits of nature and ones harmony with it. Forests, mountains, rocks, wind, earth, and sky can bring people to feel relaxed, cleansed, calm, and stronger because they are in harmony with nature, which in their cosmology has no separation.[34]

> Violet—"*Sometimes I just have to be at the ocean. I try to go as much as possible. But that is a way that I get in touch with God, with the vastness of the ocean and the waves. And I get in touch with a lot of aspects of God, not just the good aspects of water and the nutrients it brings to the body, but also the tragedy that can come with water—because it can just change on you and you get in touch with that. Sometimes the stress just walks away just rolls right off at the ocean. Nature is a good thing for me and being able to care for myself.*"

> Wanda—"*Surrounding self with pretty beautiful things—that connects me with God and people.*"

> Spirit—"*Water is healing—deep love for the ocean.*"[35]

> Rachael—"*I grow roses in my backyard—in my garden. I grow vegetables. Those I know are physically and mentally good for me. And the gardening—that is ritualistic. Yeah, the gardening—there is something too about seeing those plants grow, and working in the dirt and using your hands. It's physical exercise, but that's just healthy. It's healthy on so many levels. It's healthy because you are bending and stooping and walking around and carrying things. But also because you see seeds grow, you see the product of your work;*

---

33. See Piggue, "African American Clergy Women," 171.
34. Moodley and West, *Integrating Traditional Healing Practices*, 293–96.
35. See Piggue, "African American Clergy Women," 170–71.

What Select Neuroscientific Perspectives and Somatic Psychology

you get vegetables you can share—yeah, there is a lot of affirmation in that."[36]

In African traditional religion, an integral part of the culture represents a sum total of beliefs, attitudes, customs, methods, and established practices indicative of the worldview of the people. For Africans, there is no distinction between living and non-living, material and immaterial, natural and supernatural, conscious and unconscious. Everything is held together in unity, harmony, and in totality of life forces that maintain an equilibrium between them. Consequently, when participants mention ancestral veneration, engaging body permissions and healing, and playing indigenous instruments, they are in this sense engaging community and allowing the practice of African spirituality to facilitate healing.[37]

Throughout this work, we also realize that some of the practices African American clergy women engage in are fairly recent, based on the permission she has finally given herself to simply care for the "self" without guilt or consequence. The practice of not holding things inside and rather releasing them quickly, allowing pampering and facials, piddling, and doing nothing, preferring not to push the body too hard, making sure the doctor is seen routinely, and saying "no" are practices I contend for which African American women have had to fight. This is primarily because the nature of these practices place her center and out of reach for a time from those who have drawn from and drained her. As participants have mentioned, many of the practices came through an acquaintance with illness that forced their healing practices. It is my intent moving forward to highlight practices that reinforce healthy, caring, and fierce love for the female body.

In the next section, I share an Indigenous African healing ritual and a Buddhism-based practice. I strongly believe that this Buddhist-influenced practice is useful for African American clergy women in light of our topic of focus on care of the body. I borrow from Dr. Chanequa Walker-Barnes, who outlines the benefits of mindfulness-based stress reduction for Black women through the use of mindfulness meditation. In a section of her book *Too Heavy A Yoke: Black Women and the Burden of Strength*, entitled "Developing Self Awareness," she contends that understanding the extent of ones internalized messages and the impact on her well-being and relationships is crucial and commiserate with this study.[38] She suggests that a

---

36. See Piggue, "African American Clergy Women," 172.
37. Moodley and West, *Integrating Traditional Healing Practices*, 62.
38. See Walker-Barnes, *Too Heavy a Yoke*, 176–77, where she discusses steps in

helpful framework for cultivating self-awareness is mindfulness practice, which she shares from Symington and Symington's definition:

> The process of keeping one's mind in the present moment, while non-judgmentally detached from the potentially destructive thoughts and feelings.... [The] discipline of mindfulness, which is a form of meditation, emphasizes attentiveness to activities of the body, sensations and feelings, and mental activities.... Based upon the three pillars of presence of mind, acceptance and internal observation, their model aims to strengthen self-identity.[39]

Walker-Barnes goes on to expound upon the three pillars in this way:

> Presence of mind is a primary feature of mindfulness and is an antidote to the mindless drifting that typically characterizes the way that many people go through life. This state of mental drifting is a particular concern for the StrongBlackWoman (SBW), whose frequent responsibility and role juggling force her to remain "on the run" from the time she wakes up until the time that she goes to bed. She manages her multiple obligations by multitasking. Thus she is rarely, if ever, focused upon one activity at a time. She lacks the mental "space" needed for self-reflection and ultimately for communion with God.
>
> The second pillar, acceptance, involves learning "how to let go," accept, and not expend energy managing thoughts, feelings, and sensations that are beyond her control. This is a powerful antidote to the SBW tendency to manage distress by exerting tight control or at least attempting to exert control over her emotions and behaviors as well as those of others. It teaches the SBW to "let go" rather than "hold more tightly" when circumstances are beyond her control. And it encourages her to accept, rather than repress, feelings of vulnerability, loss, grief, and insufficiency.
>
> The third pillar is internal observation, the process whereby an individual learns to observe her internal sensations, including thoughts, feelings, and physiology. Internal observation teaches the SBW to notice and name physiological, psychological, and emotional experiences that she has grown accustomed to ignoring, minimizing or repressing, and to connect these symptoms to her tendencies toward excessive activity and responsibility. Further, it teaches her that her internal sensations are only part of who she is and that she may be capable of transcending or interrupting

---

developing mindful awareness of consequences of excessive activity Black women tend to engage.

39. Walker-Barnes, *Too Heavy a Yoke*, 179.

them. By recognizing the cycle between her hectic schedule and her physical and emotional distress, she is empowered to disrupt the cycle.[40]

I took time to extensively quote Dr. Walker-Barnes who has done what one commenter, Dr. Pamela Cooper-White, states, "meticulous" examination of the challenges Black women face and has compiled her research into an invaluable resource for many to use.

The stressors that plague African American clergy women fit conditions that are ripe for damage to the body on many levels. Consequently, the practice of mindfulness-based, stress-reduction meditation is extremely useful in healing practice as it calls one to intentionally focus and prefer the body in order to heal while allowing it to be a conduit for healing. In previous interview questions, seven of ten research participants reported that stress was a significant part of what they feel contributed to their illness.

Walker-Barnes remains concerned about the damaging effects and potential negative health outcomes connected to stress and "mindless" attention to the body as she shares the following:

> Stress is associated with a wide array of negative health outcomes among women, including headaches, stomachaches, sleep and eating disturbances, and depression. In addition to the pain distress they themselves cause, each of these symptoms is capable of exacerbating existing health problems or facilitating the development of new symptoms or diseases. . . . As the psychological impact of role strain and overload mount, Black women are especially likely to ignore, deny or repress their distress which becomes embodied in recurrent and unexplained physical problems (somatization). . . . In addition to directly resulting in symptoms of physical and emotional disease, stress is further embodied via poor coping and self-care behaviors. Women who feel stress or overwhelmed are less likely to engage in health-promoting behaviors. . . . The multiple and competing demands of their lives prevent them from establishing and maintaining healthy lifestyle habits of nutrition, exercise sleep and stress reduction.[41]

Mindfulness-based stress reduction for African-American clergy women has proven to be a very useful part of the womanist constructive framework for healing as it places her center in very dedicated spaces to address her

---

40. Walker-Barnes, *Too Heavy a Yoke*, 179.
41. Walker-Barnes, *Too Heavy a Yoke*, 67–69.

current realities. Elements of mindfulness practices are significant to this topic and in the model that will be presented, particularly as encouragement for African American clergy women to place themselves at the center and in focus for healing efforts. Deeply focused attention to the impact of thoughts and behaviors on her life will be the means through which she addresses care within the community of self.

The next section introduces a womanist constructive embodied framework for healing and the well-being of African American clergy women. It requires the type of attention and grounding found in mindfulness practice such as self-reflection, acceptance, letting go, transcendence, compassion, and empowerment, all of which will contribute to loving the self in a manner that is fierce.

7

FIERCELY Model

THE WOMANIST CONSTRUCTIVE EMBODIED framework for healing I am titling:

F   I   E   R   C   E   L   Y

It is a term inspired from Ntozake Shange's *For Colored Girls Who Have Considered Suicide*. I use it to emphasize a particular way of loving the Divine within Black women, loving the essence of Black women, and the way in which that loving should occur—*fiercely*.[1] In the form of an acrostic, a definition of "fiercely" speaks to a deep commitment and determination to prefer and protect the community of self that makes up the Black woman and, for this work, African American clergy women who may not be acquainted with fiercely loving the self. The letters signify an action that together brings awareness, love, and healing to the bodies of Black women. Fiercely stands for the following:

---

1. "I found god in myself, and I loved her, I loved her fiercely" (Shange, *For Colored Girls*, 63).

Our Bodies Are Alive

F ind her
I nvite her
E mbrace/Embolden her
R evere her
C leanse her
E mbody her
L oyal her
Y ou

Having looked closely at participant experiences and theories that offer options for construction, a model inclusive of these insights informed the design above. I repeat here that the staple of what a community of self entails is "self-literacy" and "self-love" that includes the physical body as whole and equal. Loving her with radical regard and fierceness are necessary factors for the healing desired. Essential elements of the model are outlined below.

The FIERCELY model is structured in four phases. Each letter of the word fiercely is used to guide steps and frame ritual activity to be engaged during each phase. Qualitative interview questions, responses, and assessment ground the direction and use of appropriate reparative measures. In addition, the model allows for diverse indigenous healing practices as options that resonate more readily with particular persons and experiences.

Dr. Emmanuel Lartey's model of *Postcolonializing God* offered useful language to help inform my work of also postcolonializing the African American clergy woman's body through ritual acts.

The four phases are drawn from a meaningful African ritual ceremony in which I had the privilege to participate as an Emory Global Health Institute Field Scholar during a directed study course with Dr. Emmanuel Lartey. He shares in detail the purpose and meaning of ceremonial acts engaged during the 2007 Emancipation Day Panafest celebration in Elmina, Ghana, which was a part of a research project referred to as "The Joseph Project."[2] The four structural phases are outlined in terms of Remembrance, Cleansing, Healing, and Re-Connection.

---

2. See Lartey, *Postcolonializing God*, 39–47, where he outlines the details of the 2007 Emancipation Day, Panafest Celebration, Joseph Project Launch involving a public healing ceremony that engaged "postcolonializing" God through ritual and sacred acts to heal relationships among Diasporan and Continental Africans.

Remembrance

During the liturgical ritual, hope of the healing ceremony focused on reconciling communities of diasporan and continental Africans that had been fractured, torn apart, and disconnected due to the devastating effects of the slave trade and colonial oppression.[3] As a diasporan African who was present for the ceremony, I directly experienced the value of this caliber of ritual and the healing that can be generated when the act of Sankofa[4] is engaged. In light of insights gained from neuroscience and somatic psychology, the nature of ritual and the body-mind's ability to map actions and experiences are important for inclusion in this section related to the constructive embodied model and its significance for healing. Ritual acts, I contend once more, are not to be considered simple formalities but rather opportunities for the body to map healing experiences for use at crucial points in life, in times of remembering, grieving, and celebration. It is my sense that communication within the body, as evidenced through science, would map or encode the experience into the body. However, the unseen and intangible spiritual activity would help manifest the transformation that has occurred. It is what science cannot explain but indigenous cultures have understood and practiced over time. It is the basis for inclusion of ritual acts in the model I've developed. Lartey reinforces the efficacy of ritual practice in chapter 3 of *Postcolonializing God*, stating that the presence of deeper energetic forces are an important consideration in any healing work and a powerful means of effecting change in both the seen and unseen world.[5] He goes on to share that ritual is meant to effect transformations in physical and material circumstances and in respect of healing rituals the significance of acts have to do with reversals of adverse action.[6] He shares the following from Dr. Malidoma Some's work relating to this same notion about the power of ritual practice and its ability to impact healing and change:

---

3. Lartey, *Postcolonializing God*, 39, 44–56.

4. See CGWCIE, "Power of Sankofa." Sankofa is a word in the Akan language of Ghana symbolized by the image of a bird looking backwards, meaning to "fetch what is at risk of being left behind." It supports the idea of taking from the past what is good and bringing it into the present in order to make positive progress through the benevolent use of knowledge.

5. Lartey, *Postcolonializing God*, 43.

6. Lartey, *Postcolonializing God*, 43.

Our Bodies Are Alive

> Indigenous [African] people see the physical world as more a reflection of a more complex subtler, and more lasting yet invisible entity called energy. It is as if we are shadows of a vibrant and endlessly resourceful intelligence dynamically involved in a process of continuous self-creation. . . . The material and physical problems that a person encounters are important only because they are an energetic message sent to the invisible world. Therefore, people go to the unseen energetic place to try to repair whatever damage or disturbance are being done there, knowing that if things are healed there, things will be healed here. Ritual is the principal tool used to approach that unseen world in a way that will rearrange the structure of the physical world and bring about material transformation.[7]

Unfortunately, the colonized mind has been forced to relinquish what has been life-giving and sustaining in order to assimilate beliefs and practices to that of their colonizer. "Remembering" in this ceremony was therefore the act of calling a traumatic past into a conscious, redemptive present.[8] The space was prepared very intentionally so that location, positioning on the ground, erection of the "door of return," instruments used, drums, the people present, the selection of song, and much more all played very significant and meaningful roles in conjuring the memories that needed to be evoked as a part of the ceremony.

In similar fashion the FIERCELY model uses the act of remembering to call forward the part of the community of self that has been overlooked, disconnected, and devalued as a result of varied experiences of oppression. It is relevant to include the effects of slavery, as Joy DeGruy Leary asserts in her work on Post Traumatic Slave Syndrome, wherein our bodies are the holders of trauma from centuries of pain and oppression of which our minds may not be fully aware.[9]

The first step in the remembering phase includes serious consideration of how intentional space is created for the re-valuing of the body that may be introduced to the community of the self for the first time. The focus in this phase is on creating, preparing, and entering a designated space reverently in order to facilitate and hold what will be engaged in the healing work. In this intentional space, opportunity for healing dialogue and healing acts will be supported by facilitators of the ritual practice. Reflection,

---

7. Lartey, *Postcolonializing God*, 43.
8. Lartey, *Postcolonializing God*, 62.
9. Leary, *Post Traumatic Slave Syndrome*, 116–21.

grief work, and celebration are welcomed but not forced; only the effort to be as fully present in the space as possible is encouraged. Grief work emerges as an important act, as it entails a revisiting of the incomplete developmental tasks—steps that were conceivably skipped over yet are crucial in the early life identify formation of African American clergy women.

This act of remembering includes Finding her (the body), Inviting her to the intentionally created space of healing, and ultimately Embracing her.

F—Find Her; I—Invite Her; E—Embrace Her

The avenue through which this act begins is the use of qualitative interview questions one and two: "What were early messages you received about your body?" and "How would you describe your relationship with your body in youth, young adulthood and currently?"

Data from research participants evidenced almost 100 percent that introduction to a relationship with their body early in life was absent or severely limited to mostly what to and not to do with it. Participants verified that as a result, none of them received messages that their bodies were cherished or to be valued. Example of responses included comments such as, "I grew up feeling ashamed of my body" (Wanda); "A book helped me to become more aware of it"(Autumn); "It was considered like an object rather than your person" (Jane); "The body was an enemy to control" (Frankie); "There was no explanation, I had to learn on my own and it was scary"(Lex); "It all had to do with knowing the proper ways of doing things like crossing your ankles when you sit, or holding your hands together when speaking and curtseying" (Sharon); "I observed that women's bodies were for men's pleasure and not their own" (Spirit); and, "You just didn't put yourself out there for people to notice" (Violet).

These statements demonstrate and inform my thoughts about the problem of disembodiment within the demographic of African American clergy women. Experiencing the absence of positive cultural representation and mirroring about the body, I suggest, complicates formation and adoption of a body-relationship that is valued and held equal within a community of self. Therefore, a ritual of introduction to *Find* her in an effort to reverse actions set in motion in years past is an appropriate initiation into the phase of remembering. This act is initiated by using the voice to call her forward. Sacred objects, music, drums, incense, and/or other relevant items according to the indigenous practice used can be utilized to then *Invite* her to dwell in the intentionally created space. Time is set aside to get to know her, to learn from her, and to identify what needs and questions she might have related to her body—understanding that it is within her body that the answers are held.

As the body signifies, movement into the *Embrace* stage is set. It is significant to report a summary of the findings from question three of the research tool to inform the need of a symbolic embrace at this step: "How would you describe what you were most passionate about addressing in ministry—in youth, young adulthood, and currently?" I found that early foundational interests among seven of ten participants included serving others and learning the lesson of sacrifice at a very early age. Interestingly, the three participants who did not experience major health outcomes were the same three from this question that were not oriented in their childhood to serving and sacrificing for others. Their particular responses focused on creating beautiful and comforting spaces to enjoy as a routine, enjoying physical activity without responsibility for others, and heralding self-care as a part of their relationships. A conclusion could be drawn that mapping or encoding of sacrifice and stress into the body from early ages complicates health outcomes more readily if those messages are reinforced consistently. The *Embrace* of her in this step is an acknowledgment that she may not have had the time to simply be embraced by others before having to give so much of herself away early in life. Music, touch, affirmations, movement, focused energy work, and relevant indigenous practices that build esteem and recognize worth will be the staple of this act.

R—Revere Her

In like manner the act to *Revere* is focused on the strength she has gained and who she has become in light of what may have been missing. She has still managed to rise above obstacles and achieve measures of success. Along with her were mentors and models who invested in her becoming. For most participants the report of mentorship was positive, and gratitude for what those models offered to participants was an experience of veneration at its best. In this step, acknowledging strength in her in addition to those who contributed to who she has become in ministry is a staple of this step. Libation ceremony, naming of significant persons, and recognizing all that should be acknowledged and blessed about who she is as a person, her gifts, her strengths, her beauty, her body features, and all else that deserves to be revered in the act of self-love can occur here.

Cleansing

The cleansing act in the ritual ceremony in Elmina, Ghana, came through use of symbols and acts that identified where the fractures and brokenness continued to infect the community. Identifying experiences, naming those experiences, presenting representatives, offering prayers and libation, and sacrificing for atonement were staples of this portion of the ceremony.

For the African American clergy woman, the cleansing work of dislodging what has infected her life over the years takes place in this step of the model.

C—Cleanse Her

In interview question four, participants were asked, "What are the greatest challenges you feel African American clergy women face?" From the data, at least nine themes emerged to illustrate where significant pain has been inflicted with potentially lasting effects. Earlier, I offered detailed reports of participant experiences that expound upon the following areas of noted challenge: bias against women, mistrust by others and among one another, imposed requirements for acceptance into ministry, setting appropriate boundaries, lack of support, self-acceptance/being true to the self, psychological trauma, religious oppression, and theological distortions. From the data received, I report that these challenges remain critical in the lives of African American clergy women and have been potential conduits for unhealthy self-identity, poor self-esteem, and negative health outcomes. Subsequent questions number six and seven speak to the experience of negative health outcomes. Nine of ten participants reported having experienced and feeling confident that particular behavioral patterns of imbalance and negative health outcomes had some correlation to one another.

As a result, *Cleanse* her begins with identifying the impact challenges have had on clergy women and their physical bodies. In addition to this question is asking how practices passed down through modeling have manifested in their ministry paradigm and subsequently through their health by following the model. At least seven of the ten women reported that they believe an imbalance in use of the models they followed contributed to negative health outcomes in their lives. Many named stress as a major factor and contributor to expressed medical conditions in their bodies.

In like manner to the ceremonial ritual of cleansing, the work in this step includes the use of symbols and the act of identifying where the pain of these experiences are located within the bodies of women participating in the ritual. Particular attention is given to where she feels the pain has settled within her body and has attempted to infect her community of self. Identifying experiences, naming the impact of those experiences, and calling upon representatives to stand with her as the cleansing work begins sets this step in motion. Subsequently, prayers are offered—along with libation, the ritual act of purification, and atoning—as women release or dislodge messages and pain that they have mapped within their body. Items to use in this rite are informed by the indigenous spiritual practice chosen.

Healing

This phase in the ritual ceremony at Elmina ushered in a new era of emotional wellness, repairing legacies of disease. Confession and requests for pardon was enacted and maintained that a resolution to work to ensure that such inhumanity of the slave trade was never again to be repeated.

E—Embody Her

As clearing and cleansing occurs, room is made for healing within the community in this step. In the case of African American clergy woman seeking to be united with her community of self, a ceremony of release is engaged here. More specifically, ritual structure, confession, pardon/forgiveness, and resolution are utilized in this step. Interview questions five, six, and seven aid in the exploration of behaviors and experiences that may have been counterproductive to healthy development during certain phases in life. An intentional time of discovery and confession regarding her own participation in the destruction of her body is explored. Subsequently, forgiveness in dialogue with her body and a commitment to compassion, kindness, and grace for her body is acknowledged. Empathy is also offered as transformation and change in her actions occur over time. Embracing practices that are hospitable to her community of self and that are balanced in healthy ways is the focus of this step. Additionally, affirmations, a re-valuing, and a re-naming of her community of self will be a catalyst for

FIERCELY Model

greater *Embodied* function. Preparing a covenant plan of care in writing for her life as she continues to carry the burden of ministry is another staple within this step. Incense, music, drumming, and relevant symbolism are appropriate practices as well. To complete this step, a washing ritual that acknowledges contrition, spiritual healing, and well-being within the community can be an important engagement.

Reconnection

The act in this phase of the ceremony was to bring fractured communities into touch with each other again. In the ritual ceremony at Elmina, the acknowledgment that unatoned violence can leave the spirit restless and disturbed required ritual in order to end what had gone unaddressed for years. Allowing the spirit to rest through this process of healing served as a beginning process of reconciliation and rapprochement between continental and diasporan Africans.

Restoring to balance her community of self is celebrated in this phase and marked with symbolic transition into embodied existence.

L—Loyal Her

This step includes acts of connection and re-connection with the body, bringing into focus the final interview question about how her healing practices are engaged. A step toward *Loyalty* to her has already begun because there is purpose in her decision to engage healing practice. Protection and preference will be defined in addition to exploring meaningful rituals that convey how loyalty to the decision to love herself fiercely will be maintained. Finally, a covenant design crafted in a way that can be sustained and revisited for continued healing is encouraged. This would include a commitment to reflective processes that promote self-literacy and self-relationship in ways she can manage.

Y—You

This step literally punctuates that no one other than *You* can ensure care of your body in the manner in which it deserves. A body scan of the parts that make you, *you*, is acknowledged in ways that are meaningful to participants as they engage the last act of this healing ritual. Articulation of the fact that *you* are the Goddess inside that you love is shared, and the use of mirrors will be a helpful tool as participants map an image within the body for reference at a later time.

For African American clergy women who are learning to love the community of self *FIERCELY!*

8

A Womanist Theological Reflection
The Cannanite Woman Archetype
(Matthew 15:21–28)

IN THIS SECTION, I offer a theological reflection on the Canaanite woman and the archetype she represents for women of color in the fight against oppression. She in many ways loves fiercely and embodies a regard for the self that is worthy of attention as well as consideration of exemplary modeling. Two womanist trailblazers, Renita Weems and Phillis Sheppard, offered useful methods of literary, text, and biblical criticism for this analysis. Weems offers respected scholarship and expertise as a biblical scholar in order to give voice to the many voiceless women in biblical literature. In her books *Just a Sister Away* and *Battered Love*, she powerfully challenges male perspectives of the text and aids women in identifying a more liberative message related to their experiences. Weems "attempts to combine the best of the fruits of feminist biblical criticism with its passion for reclaiming and reconstructing the stories of biblical women, along with the best of the Afro-American oral tradition, with its gift for story-telling and its love for drama."[1] Weems also "builds upon insights of gender criticism, literary studies, studies of the erotic, and sociological and ideological analyses to illuminate the relationship between biblical literature and its social setting."[2] Her encouragement to engage the task of being an "ethically responsible

---

1. Weems, *Just a Sister Away*, ix.
2. Weems, *Battered Love*, 5–6.

exegete that helps readers find ways of understanding how literature both plays on our greatest fears and taps into our noblest ideals"[3] remained a constant reminder in my reflection to follow. Finally, I have attempted to follow a similar goal of encouraging readers "to claim their rights to differ with authors, especially those marginalized by the texts, whether the worlds that authors place us in are indeed worth inhabiting."[4] Building on a quote by Michael Foucault, she further emphasizes that "it's always worth re-examining the biblical metaphors we have inherited from the past to see to what extent, if at all they remain relevant for talking about God and human existence."[5] I also use what Phillis Sheppard refers to as "hermeneutical re-reading of the biblical texts for examples of the voices of those who have been marginalized, who are models for inspired resistance to oppression as well as a re-reading our inherited religious traditions for liberative readings that have been overlooked in earlier readings."[6] These have been most useful in this reflection on the Canaanite woman narrative. Lartey's concept of "post-colonializing God" comes to be a very relevant partner in critique and examination of this text in light of constructing an empowering framework for pastoral theological healing approaches.

The Canaanite woman narrative offers a model that draws attention and respect to the concerns of women while seeming to avoid internalizing dehumanizing marginalization. She also demonstrates a manner of loving fiercely that can only be rooted in her understanding of self-love that is inclusive of what and who she loves as a part of her community of self. I am most focused on her ability to employ strategies rooted in an understanding of her right to well-being, not rooted in a particular religion but in her value as a human person, deserving of dignity, respect, and healing.

For the purpose of this focus, I will reflect upon several strategies the Canaanite woman uses to address oppression in a way that helps to frame womanist constructive thought.

I began with concern for African American clergy women who fight the fight of oppression and find themselves broken and unable to function optimally due to the toll it can take on their bodies and will. In light of greater insights related to the concept of body mapping, I questioned what it was about the Canaanite woman that allowed her to seemingly avoid

3. Weems, *Battered Love*, 9.
4. Weems, *Battered Love*, 10.
5. Weems, *Battered Love*, 10.
6. Sheppard, "Dark Goodness Created in the Image of God," 5–28.

internalizing messages ascribed to her and her people in a way that did not paralyze her efforts and advocacy. They were a despised group, marginalized, disdained, and reproached, yet she did not allow those biases to deter her from what she felt was right and just. It stands to reason, based upon the concept of body mapping, that given the rejection and labeling of her people, it would be an appropriate claim that negative energetic forces associated with those underlining messages of unworthiness could easily have become a part of her identity. They did not however seem to find enough ground per se to settle within her body and fortify the belief that she was unworthy. The Canaanite woman maintained a level of sagacity that kept her apparent self-love and true essence intact—so much so that Jesus would eventually "see" her and esteem her highly.

This biblical vignette highlights a useful constructive womanist approach to addressing oppressive systems while at the same time maintaining a radical regard and love for the "self." This approach understands that at the heart of a womanist framework is a resistance-oriented stance that serves as a way to resist being excluded, dehumanized, and invisible. In this biblical vignette, the Canaanite woman is driven by her passion, vision, and focus on attaining liberation and healing on behalf of another with no voice, but who knew she deserved life—despite oppressive forces that would suggest otherwise. Important in this work is attention to the almost imperceptible fact that inherent within her efforts is a regard she also affords herself, something we have seen in this study that African American clergy women often neglect in their efforts to balance care for others.

I reflect upon the story of the Canaanite woman in which she challenges culturally-constructed narratives latent with negative messages meant to limit her in various ways. As one consigned to a particular role in history, the Canaanite woman's victory offers insight into practical means of challenging oppressive systems, surviving through those systems and living free and aware though the systems remain. Dr. Carroll Watkins Ali offers definitions for survival and liberation which are useful throughout this discussion and even more so in helping to identify that in which the Canaanite woman is grounded and draws from in pursuit of healing. We will recognize these in the Canaanite woman's approach, posture, and state of mind throughout the vignette. Watkins Ali defines "survival" as "the ability to resist systematic oppression and genocide, and to recover the self, which entails a psychological recovery from abuse and dehumanization of political oppression and exploitation as well as recovery of African heritage, culture, and values that are repressed during slavery."[7] Watkins Ali defines "liberation" as "total freedom from all kinds of oppression for African descendants of slaves and the ability of African Americans as a people to determine and engage in the process of transformation of the dominant oppressive culture through political resistance."[8]

The Canaanite woman uses such an approach by learning the rules and categories of the oppressive system she faced as a means of subversion through resistance to challenge the very systems that sought to reinforce oppressive existentialist claims. In conversation with Jesus, she demonstrated strategies for developing liberating action that yielded life and freedom for those in need of God's intervention.

Strategies

Three strategies emerge from my reflection over the Canaanite woman's encounter against an oppressive system. (1) She located and grounded herself within the encounter, identifying the issues inherent within to include her lineage/heritage, her daughter and daughter's illness, her value, her entitlement to well-being, available healing, risks, and what her strategic efforts would be. (2) She maintained love as a driving force for action. (3) She utilized self-literacy as a compliment to literacy related to the oppressive system in which she found herself. She prepared through awareness not only of the social, political, religious laws, and customs but also through her own sense of emotional awareness and psychological grounding that would inform her choice of how to engage the encounter—not in reaction but from a position of power.

Strategy 1—Locating Herself

The Canaanite woman's interaction with Jesus suggested a boldness rooted not only in intellectual knowledge but also in spiritual knowing regarding her importance and rightful place as an heir deserving of healing interventions in the life of her daughter and self. That type of knowing was deeply spiritual knowing, revealed by God, and not mere convention. It was such that oppressive existentialist's claims of superiority were understood but

---

7. Watkins Ali, *Survival and Liberation*, 2.
8. Watkins Ali, *Survival and Liberation*, 2.

A Womanist Theological Reflection

not accepted. In this manner her people, a gentile group who were constrained by culturally constructed demeaning messages, were relegated to status of "last." However, the Canaanite woman, who was well informed, began the use of a subversive strategy in invoking her understanding of the lineage from which she had come to call to remembrance the reason why she had a right to stand firm with confidence in conversation with Jesus. In her first request, she draws upon her relevant heritage among gentile women, who were participants in aiding Jesus' arrival to the earth (Rahab and Ruth were both gentile women).

Likewise, African American clergy women in the spirit of Sankofa should remember that their heritage does not begin in a state of oppression and that there is always much more that informs one's sense of relevance.[9] In recognizing and affirming her lineage despite the cultural norm that excluded her people, even from the intervention of God's healing, the Canaanite woman seems to insert herself into the center of the conversation and literally transforms the experience of being the object of another's abuse into a subject in control of her own destiny. By standing firm and not backing down when initially no answer came, the Canaanite woman demonstrated confidence in her right to ask and to be heard. She maintained and believed in her value.

Strategy 2—Love as a Driving Force

In true womanist fashion, the Canaanite woman approached Jesus on behalf of another. She stood fervent and sound in her role as advocate for one who could not speak for herself and was motivated by a love similar to God's. Further, she demonstrated that despite messages assigned to her oppressed culture, she would take the risk against institutionalized norms to ask for what was just regardless of the possible outcome of harm and/or humiliation to her. Her love for the other grounded her efforts as any advocate would on behalf of a greater cause. She looked to protect life for the next generation.

---

9. See CGWCIE, "Power of Sankofa." Sankofa is a word in the Akan language of Ghana symbolized by the image of a bird looking backwards, meaning to "fetch what is at risk of being left behind." It supports the idea of taking from the past what is good and bringing it into the present in order to make positive progress through the benevolent use of knowledge.

Strong convictions, a love that mirrored God's, and focus that kept her centered on a greater purpose continued to fuel her efforts to insure a chance at life. Love remained central in the act of resistance by serving as an act of resistance.

Strategy 3—Utilizing Self-Literacy and Literacy About Systems

The Canaanite woman's resistance to Jesus's silence yields a retort that is less than acceptable and reinforced the existential claims of superiority as he reminds her that he had not yet come to her people, engaging in dialogue latent with the vanity of empty rituals. He did this at the expense of observing covenant commandments of compassion, justice, and righteousness, which the Canaanite woman raised for his consideration. To that point, her strategy of subversive resistance had been more a practice of internal reflection that informed her resolute stance and persistent agency. Her focus and commitment to what was not apparent in Jesus's actions but glaring in hers—through prophetic protests against social injustice and the vanity of empty rituals—aided her in determination to continue the dialogue. She did this with wisdom and knowledge of the orthodoxy of the covenant that was referenced. She was knowledgeable and well-informed about the details enough to speak clearly and intelligently about the rules inherent within it.

In her response she subversively uses this knowledge and an understanding of its conventional observances of oppressive laws to challenge the oppressive system to basically follow their own rules. She did not allow emotionalism to overtake her or to cause her to become defensive. She functioned from the posture of a self-literate and actualized self who understood her value, worth, and identity along with the rules and categories of the Jewish system, all of which motivated her to remain focused on her path toward liberation and healing. She had studied their laws, customs, culture, and language in order to be well-prepared in conversation that would lead to God's intervention. In her judicious retort, she uses Jesus's language and excuse by expanding upon it in order to crystallize the hypocrisy therein as well as to highlight her deeper knowledge and hermeneutic regarding what the covenant truly meant. Jesus was then called into remembering what he was there for. The strategy was somewhat parabolic, as Jesus often used, in an attempt to make obvious that which seemed obscure. Against this strategy, it seemed there was no further challenge, as it appeared to call Jesus

A Womanist Theological Reflection

into remembrance of all he stood for and what was actually fair, compassionate, and righteous. He was disarmed and then willing, as the divinity in him rose to the surface to offer what was just. This Canaanite woman, if she had nothing else, she determined to be educated and informed.

Within this vignette, I recognize and suggest that the Canaanite woman represents a construction of the self, an archetype that functioned at a degree of holistic health uncommon for a woman of her time and social and cultural status. She had somehow mastered what many take significant pains to achieve. If we return to the definitions Watkins Ali offers, the Canaanite woman as a part of a despised group who suffered regularly under oppressive laws and cultural bias seems to have transcended the binding labels and messages.

An appropriate lens through which I have chosen to view the strategies of the Canaanite woman is the concept of postcolonializing.[10] In each of the strategies, the Canaanite woman passionately opposes domination and definition at the hands of the Israelites. As a way of postcolonializing her location and/or status in strategy 1, she invokes the fact that God had been present, active, and involved in affirming her value and worth over the ages, even to the extent of choosing her people as conduits through which Jesus would become an earthly being. Her shout of, "Have mercy on me, Lord Son of David!" points to her well-informed lineage. Thus she began a subversive strategy by invoking her understanding of that lineage calling Jesus to remembrance about the reason she had a right to stand firm and confident in conversation with him. By remembering her heritage among gentile women, who participated in aiding Jesus's arrival to the earth, the Canaanite woman placed herself at the center of the conversation and

---

10. See Lartey, *Postcolonializing God*, xiii, where he explains use of a reformulation of the source word postcolonial in adjective and verb form. "As an adjective, 'postcolonializing' qualifies the divine, offering thoughts describing an aspect of the nature of God. . . . The study is of ways in which God may be seen to be present and active in the world . . . as involved and in interaction with humans. God is seen as one who, in keeping with the divine nature, acts to decolonize, diversify and promote counter-hegemonic social conditions. As a verb, 'postcolonializing' articulates the nature, acts and activities of communities, leaders or people who seek to establish communities of faith or else who produce or provide regularly or occasionally rituals or ceremonies that, reflecting the decolonizing nature of the divine, are in plural form, diverse in character and which subvert and overturn the hegemonic conditions established through colonialism creating forms of spiritual engagement that more truly reflect categories of thought and life that emanate from an African, rather than a European, way of being and thinking."

literally transforms the experience of being the object of another's abuse into a subject in control of her own destiny.

In strategy 2, the act of advocating on behalf of another is the epitome of the mission for which Jesus had actually come to the earth. Through love, the Canaanite woman lived more fully into that mission in the moment by sacrificing and seeking healing for someone other than herself. In the sense of postcolonializing, she presents God and reflects the decolonizing nature of the divine in order to create a form of spiritual engagement that more truly reflects the purpose of why her request was made.[11] Her advocacy made room for that which made sense—love to persist in the face of Jesus' prophetic protests and support of empty ritual practices that would aid in death rather than life. She exegetically dismantled his narrative through a hermeneutic based in love, thus decolonizing useless tradition in the face of need.

In strategy 3, postcolonializing in a similar fashion was engaged by the Canaanite woman through subversion of the hegemonic conditions established through colonialism.[12] Her retort fits what Lartey posits is a creation of spiritual engagement that more truly reflects categories of thought and life that are truer than what the oppressive system attempts to impose.[13] Through subversion, the Canaanite woman demonstrated first that she was literate in her understanding of the domination system's rules and categories. She had studied their laws, customs, culture, and language in order to be well prepared and grounded. She used Jesus's language and excuse by expanding upon it in order to crystallize the hypocrisy therein as well as to highlight her deeper knowledge and hermeneutic regarding what the covenant truly meant. Through all of these efforts the Canaanite woman emerged seemingly strong, satisfied, and whole, not to mention relieved that her daughter was healed. I reiterate here that the archetype she offers is one that holds significant power, balance, clarity, and health from which African American clergy women might draw when engaging oppression that remains a part of the everyday life of this group of women.

The conversation of self-care and Black women's health persists as a major concern because Black women continue to experience health challenges at alarming rates. Because the conversation continues, I will continue

11. Lartey, *Postcolonializing God*, xiii.
12. Lartey, *Postcolonializing God*, xiii.
13. Lartey, *Postcolonializing God*, xiii.

A Womanist Theological Reflection

as an invested stakeholder and spiritual care practitioner who understands their plight. Through this work, my goal has been to stimulate awareness and interests in what are underrepresented parts of the dialogue. Those underrepresented parts are insights gained from what womanist theology always grounds, what the body has to communicate, what neuroscience illuminates, and what indigenous spiritual practices have offered over time, despite hegemonic attempts to discredit its influence.

Continuing to shed light on contributing factors that inform the problems facing African American clergy women and the challenges associated with her manner of relating to her body is critical and will remain the impetus for my work until my work is done.

Appendix

African American Clergy Women Interview Responses

What follows is a compilation of all participant responses using pseudonyms.

1. What were early messages you received about your body?

    Wanda—"I grew up feeling kind of ashamed of my body. I had brothers, one bathroom and the house had one bedroom. We slept in the same bed so had to be fully clothed at all times. I never saw my mother's body either. She made it so that neither of us could see each other, so I thought something was wrong with my body."

    Violet—"A couple of things—one you had to sit with your legs closed. You had to be clean. You didn't wear shorts. My mom was from one conservative denomination and my dad was from another so there were certain things that you just didn't do and because there were a large number of girls in my family and only a few boys, privacy was important to us. So you were supposed to take care of yourself. I remember my grandmother calling us fast tail girls. I never knew why she called us that; Fast tail girls sort of made me think of those who were very fresh and promiscuous and put themselves out there for boys to touch.

African American Clergy Women Interview Responses

We never did any of that sort of thing. She probably said it because she was a fast tail woman. She always did love men better than she did women. But yeah we were supposed to be clean, were supposed to sit properly, not wear clothes that were suggestive. Of course I was very skinny so I didn't have to worry about anybody wanting me. My younger sisters were much more well-developed than I was. So it made me very protective of my body and of my younger sisters. There were places you didn't go and people you didn't hang around; people that were known to be more 'free' with themselves. So I became like- a word I would use is prudish, very reserved, and 'school mannish'. A lot of people thought I was a teacher. Yeah, there were certain ways you walked and didn't walk. I was raised in a way that said—you just didn't put yourself out there for people to notice or be drawn."

Autumn—"I was too tall, too skinny, was black like my daddy, so couldn't wear bright colors—like red lipstick, fingernail polish. I don't know if I devalued my body in any way but I didn't necessary value it from the beginning. All those messages were subtle. I worked at a young age and I was always very active. I didn't value it in terms of taking care of myself. I did not cherish it because those were not the kind of messages I received. The book—Our Bodies Our Selves—helped me to become more aware of my body during the time when I entered college. So my body became alive when I was in college."

Yvette—"I never got teased about my body, but it came because of skin color. Being one of the darkest girls in my 1st grade class—I received a lot of jabbing from my classmates. Kids were really mean. I was always slender, so nothing about the body, but about the persona. Within the black community there was also segregation because of skin color, like the Jim Crow South. My house was full of love and never commented on it. So the messages outside were kinda that I was not good enough, that I was different. Teachers helped me to overcome that because they reinforced that I was a bright student. My intelligence helped me through the trials of this time. Parents never made a big deal, but Dad called me bow-legged child because they were like his. Mom lamented about combing my hair because it was so thick."

African American Clergy Women Interview Responses

Spirit—"The most prominent was that I had a big behind, so most of my nicknames in childhood from neighborhood kids either referenced my behind, which was I guess large in comparison to the rest of my body, I was a pretty skinny kid; Or they would reference another body part that was distinct. As a small child, skin color was never an issue. My parents were professionals, affirming of black history, Afro-centric, so anything related to skin color for me probably didn't emerge until high school and I was sort of in the middle of the light skin, dark skin issue—not too much of either. Sex was a no, no of course. Touching yourself was a no, no. We became involved in church and everything sexual was for grown folks, marriage, procreation, etc. I remember having the birth control pill talk before I went to college, which was—if you want to have sex, let me know."

Frankie—"It was through the community that I knew I had a body because attention was drawn to it when me and friends moved our bodies in certain ways and were reprimanded from community women. So we were made aware that we had one. When I was younger a classmate who was very developed, dark and heavy, was made fun of by others and me. I was reprimanded and shamed in front of others for it. Then after school in a fight with the classmate, I was teased by boys because my shirt fell and my breasts were bare—so I was made conscious of it. Another message was that the body was vulnerable and men could do something to it. I got that from watching abuse of my mother by men physically. If anger was present, fear came because that abuse could happen to your body. Menstrual cycle and other girl things made me aware of my body. Pentecostal church experience in college caused dissonance when messages about the flesh being bad or negative began to surface. Holiness was connected to body restrictions, abstaining from sex—gave impression that body was now 'bad,' which was not the case in my experience before. I began praying to bring the body under subjection; the body became an enemy I needed to control."

Jane—"Your body wasn't really talked about, so as I grew into womanhood, others would talk about what that meant, usually from a negative perspective, not positive. In church around 10 years old, I did my own reading biblically—I learned that my body was the temple of God and that it was holy and sacred and should be treated with respect. From parents—you just didn't talk about the body. It was usually equated with sex, so you just didn't. You learned about the body in terms of physicality in health class and it was considered like an object rather than your person."

Sharon—"That I was freckled; was disappointed because of them. One grandmother tried to get rid of them. I never got positive or negative messages about my complexion or hair. My other grandmother worried about the kitchen in the back of the head/hair. I was told that girls should walk straight. I learned to walk with a book on my head. I had to hold my hands together when speaking and curtsey. I had to cross my ankles etc. . . . It all had to do with knowing the proper ways of doing things."

Lex—"That your body was a private place, private areas, parts that no one was to touch. And you could not ask questions about your body. It was bad to touch. There was no explanation about breasts, puberty, or starting your cycle. I had to learn on my own and it was scary."

Rachael—"I shouldn't defile my body. Parents were concerned that we had four sisters, we were not to be engaged in sex while we were young—concerned with shame and reputation; expectation that we would eat vegetables. Healthy eating would make our bodies healthy. We had cod liver oil a lot and every winter, our family had dose of castor oil. So in that regard we were taught to take care of our bodies. We worked physically because I grew up on a farm. There wasn't a lot of talk about using our bodies physically and keeping our bodies physically fit. But it was definitely communicated that you don't just let your body go. You use your body physically—you can't be slothful—have to be doing something with your body."

2. How would you describe your relationship with your body—in your youth, young adulthood, and currently?

Wanda—"It was really detached as a youth. I didn't claim it as my own, if I had that language. I just maintained it. Didn't start cycle until 13, but did not have any conversation with my mother about how that was to happen so faked it because others had theirs. I was shocked when it finally came and didn't know what to do: Was sent in bathroom alone to figure out everything. At a later time when I put socks in my bra it *finally sparked conversation with my mother who affirmed that I was fine just the way I was. No conversation about sex however, so I didn't know anything. I had not seen a man's body or barely a woman's body. I had to figure that out also. Because my spouse was gentle it helped me to get comfortable with my body. Currently I am very attuned to my body and am clear when changes are occurring. Not afraid of it."*

Violet—*"In my youth, I was very very skinny, so dressing out for gym was very hard, because I had long skinny legs and arms, so I was somewhat ashamed of my body. All my siblings were a bit different in body shape than me so I was ashamed of my body as a teenager. One of my brothers laughed at my knees because he saw them as knots on my skinny legs, so that reinforced that you don't let anyone see that. Going on to college in the first year I gained weight, so then I got the attention of boys. So from young adulthood to mid-adulthood I got attention and could turn heads. But I still wouldn't show my body. The way I dressed would be to cover so nobody really knew my shape because I would wear clothes to camouflage it so you wouldn't be able to tell how I looked. Then because of an illness my body was disfigured. So for about ten years I should have been proud of my body, because it was probably the time in my life when it was close to perfect, but it had been such a difficult time growing up that I hadn't gotten to the point of being able to appreciate my body until the illness showed up. And that just messed it up. And so I'm an older adult now. I wasn't ashamed of the disfigurement of the illness because I was grateful to be alive, so that didn't bother me. But I think I didn't recover from the childhood messages of 'you had to be a certain way or don't do a certain thing' until after my mom died. Interesting thing that it wasn't until after she died did I start to become free in my being able to appreciate 'Me' as a woman. And so at that point my body was still in pretty good shape. This year, I've started the senior citizen decline. So the body is going downhill (laughing). That firmness was still here last year and year before, but this year—no. So it seems that I have not had many years of loving my body and I know that I am blessed to be alive because I have been challenged with my illness recurring over the years. Currently my relationship with my body is good. I am exercising a lot more now than I ever did. I appreciate my body and I feel freer in me to be a Me and comfortable being a woman. I haven't always been comfortable being a woman and what I mean by that is I hadn't always* been comfortable wearing the pretty, frilly things, and not a lot of bright colors partly because I would not mix colors very well, but I wouldn't wear the girly, frilly things because that would have acknowledged I was a woman and attracted the guys. It's taken me a long time to get to that place and I really do think it had something to do with my mom's death. I think I got some freedom when she died."

Autumn—"In my youth I received messages that my body was imperfect and then when I became a young adult, I thought I was ugly. As I matured and was finally getting in touch with things about my body, I began to realize that I really wasn't ugly. I'm not too skinny, men were attracted to me. I then felt a sense of my own sassiness. I went through a period of real insecurity from young adulthood to mid. I remember feeling like an ugly duckling and questioning whether I was valued. That came from falling in love and being sexually active. Depending on how a man treated me acceptance/rejection that also played into how I felt about my body. Once a Christian in young adulthood I fell in love with Psalm 139—it affirmed who I was—'knit in my mother's womb' like the idea of physically being made by design—everything about me is just right. So that today I affirm myself all the time because I am by design. I believe it is important to take care of myself.—Getting plenty of rest, exercise, eating right, not abusing my body. I decided to live celibate. It was a spiritual decision while doing ministry. It has meant health—emotionally, physically, no threat of rejection etc. No one can play games with my body."

Yvette—"Back to how I was different, when people point things out to me I noticed that I had thin legs, a big nose but overall I really didn't think too much about it prior to that. My self-awareness—I had a lot of personality and was affirmed by my uncle and friends. As I matured, I left for college and my bow legs caught attention. There were incidences after I married. I met my husband in college. After five years of marriage—he had a vile temper and would do name calling and some of the things he would say to me heightened my awareness of who I was—but then I could not look at myself in the mirror. It wasn't until later that I started making myself look at me, the whole person, and began to like the person who was there. Self-esteem was something I had to grow because of stigma from early on and the subsequent marriage relationship.

African American Clergy Women Interview Responses

That is when it became apparent to me that I had to have some sense of who I was and that if there was something I disliked, I had the option to change it. Currently that is how I would describe it today."

Spirit—*"As an early youth I would have been considered a tom boy, some of this points to gender and embodiment. Stereotypically I liked boy stuff. I was athletic, I liked fishing and hunting. I observed that women's bodies were for men's pleasure and not your own. So you really didn't have a sense that your body fully belonged to yourself. I think because people really didn't talk about it directly. Most of the good stuff I got about my body was related to eating and health. My family was vegetarian. It was a part of their Afri-centrism. Eating healthy was good. In youth, physical health was important. I was athletic and was a dancer. So that was always encouraged in some ways. But it was always the gender and sexuality stuff that was a little more disconnected. Introductions to that were conversations with your girlfriends or street friends. That's where you learned stuff, that's where you explored, that's where you would sneak and watch porn so it didn't come directly from adults. Introduction to your menstrual cycle, which I was a little late relative to my friends, you kind of learned your body through those experiences and how you negotiate and navigate that in middle school.*

I think young adulthood interestingly was a little more tumultuous for two reasons: One, conservative, evangelical theology renounced the body, so there was not that affirmation of the body. There was that whole Platonic split between body and spirit, the flesh is evil, you were going to hell if you engaged anything to do with the flesh, but in terms of gender and sexuality, it was almost always negative outside the context of marriage. So it wasn't until later in young adulthood in undergrad and grad school that you really start to ask questions about some of those things and become kind of more aware of your body and relationship with it, and start to say, 'How the hell can everything be wrong?' Why would God create people with hormones that you don't have anything to do with; you didn't choose it; its part of your natural evolution and development and then say don't do that? Now that's ridiculous. Masturbation was the biggest sin in young adulthood and youth. It wasn't until later I found out that boys and men don't seem to have any issues with it. They do it days, nights, weekends, and whenever they feel like it and it's fine. Nobody is reprimanding them for it. But women we have to deal with a lot of guilt and a lot of shame and I distinguish the two because I think for women, guilt can easily turn to shame because it can become a part of one's own self-identity and self-definition—it's not just behavioral anymore which is something you repent for and discharge. It's now who I am and I begin asking questions like what's wrong with me as a person or biologically. So seminary and of course Womanism helped me to get liberated from some conservative evangelical views of my own body and embodiment.

Now as an adult, I think I have a great relationship with my body. I know my body and my body's rhythms. That came through a pretty arduous journey with physical conditions related to stress and hell and unhealthy relationships which worsened the condition along with unhealthy food intake in a certain period of life. But in a strange way and positive way it put me in touch with my body—helped me to understand my body's rhythm and pay attention to pain in my body in particular kinds of ways. I ignored my body for some time in order to complete school. Now I am peri-menopausal which puts you in touch with your body in other particular kind of ways.

Sexual evolution of course, being comfortable with my body sexually claiming who I am and loving it, that I am fearfully and wonderfully made, knowing that there is nothing ontologically wrong with me. I am now reading writers that help me understand my spirituality in relation to my embodiment."

Frankie—*"In youth my relationship with my body was abstract. I wasn't clear what it could do. Spin the bottle type games suggest doing something with it in adolescence—like a kiss—no real connection with the action. Weight—Mother would try to warn against getting heavy, fear was developed about what weight means related to body. Teen years—I was popular, had friends but prided self on 'Not' having sex even though some friends did. So I used my body as a tool to communicate a stance. I had surgery in youth that prevented me from fun so I was unhappy at my body for restricting life events. Today I have more of an appreciation for the body. It's more lip service though because I lack enough action that can preserve it. It is an amazing thing to behold. It can regenerate and heal itself with correct thoughts and communication. A medical condition that caused other complications within my body has caused me to come into more relationship and intimacy with my body. Overall thought—Medically, spiritually, and sexually at this stage the body is a great thing."*

African American Clergy Women Interview Responses

Jane—"Not sure I was very conscious about it then, but I was always very skinny. I was always comparing my body to sisters, family and friends wishing for more of one thing or another. So my body was too skinny, unattractive, etc. . . . As I went to college, and began putting on weight, I got hips and was noticed by others. I became self-conscious then because others were looking and making assessments. As I've gotten older, I look at my body more through a health lens. My weight often drives how I feel. I am most comfortable at a certain weight. It's more about wanting to be healthy. Mom has this thing about weight, so comments when she sees me. Now it's not about being attractive but healthy."

Sharon—"As a youth, I tried to be attractive, cute, thin, wear my hair a certain way. I don't remember if I had any particular relationship with my body. As a young adult it was more about being pregnant and a parent. I think I came into myself and felt most attractive when I was a young adult. I felt attractive after I had my children. As an older person my relationship is one of disgust. Not because it's not attractive but my interest is more about my health and how I feel rather than what it looks like; and I haven't felt well in my body. I wish I had appreciated the health that I had because I was very healthy as a young adult. I was a runner and was strong, had excellent memory, my mind was good. I'm seeing myself on the decline as an older person and I am not happy about that at all. So it's a source of aggravation. It hurts—arthritis issues. I can't eat what I want to eat; if I do it causes discomfort because of a certain medical condition."

Lex "In youth very awkward and not really knowing anything about my body. In young adulthood—reading books, finding out what different body parts were. It was just taboo, so you just didn't talk about it. I began to research on own in young adult life. I was always inquisitive about why things work the way they do. My cycle prompted more study. I knew nothing. I wondered if I was going to die or bleed to death. The generation before me had the same experience, but didn't do it differently. My PE coach gave me a book. Now, I might say I'm more attuned to my body, but still having struggles because I was never taught anything about touch, exploration, etc. Still trying to learn what I like, but it's ok."

African American Clergy Women Interview Responses

Rachael—"As a child and young adolescent, I thought I was physically strong and smarter than my male siblings. So that's one thing I thought about my body. I thought that it was useful. An instrument of who I was. I think that came from growing up on a farm. I thought at one point when I was an early teenager, that I started to become conscious of my body and thought I was too heavy. I guess as I was entering adolescence or teenage years I wanted to look attractive. So I dressed in ways that I thought were attractive. I did the hot pants thing, tried to hide from mother how hot they were. I remember my body being attractive by the time I was a senior in high school and flaunting it in purples and lively colors, on into college. I still thought I was smart; though there were not enough messages about how to balance the attention that I got for my body with how intelligent I was. So I was conflicted and confused about that in some ways, probably well into my young adult life. I continued to care for my body. I think the messages I got about what I ate, stayed with me. I think they still do and still have; although I have not been as conscientious. I am a vegetable lover, and so probably because I like vegetables and because of those messages I am not heavy, heavy. So I walk and aerobics now and as a young adult I did those things as well. So in terms of caring for my body now, I think those messages came through and they continue and continue. I appreciate my body and know if I don't care for it, it will not be there for me to be. In terms of relating to my body and my sexuality, I had to learn—had to decipher how to do that. It was difficult and late and challenging and I was fully adult by the time I was comfortable in understanding myself as a sexual person. So in regard to relating to myself and to my body as, or to sexuality as an element of my embodiment, I don't think that there were places that helped me to navigate and learn about that."

3. How would you describe what you are most passionate about addressing in ministry? (1) in your youth, (2) in your adulthood, and (3) currently?

Wanda—"When I was younger I thought a woman could only be a pastor's wife. I hung with older women in the community. Aspired to be a pastor's wife because they were very loving and attentive and they sang. So my passion was to emulate the older women—they were like my friends and they would give me all their time and wisdom. I didn't have a lot of girlfriends. I wanted to be good model for my younger sister when she was born. In college I felt a call to ministry but had not seen women in that capacity, so didn't know what to do with it. It was a tug inside. I moved into a phase of being authentic with people after praying with a friend who didn't think I struggled with anything. I would hold Bible study and encourage authenticity. Now I'm passionate about people knowing they can be comforted by my presence and about teaching others to do the same."

Violet—"*I think when I was a young person, I just wanted to get to know Jesus. Well let me say it another way. We were raised in the church so it was very much a part of my life. I taught Sunday school, I ushered in the church, my mom and dad raised us there, so there was never a question of whether you were going to go to church. I actually grew up thinking everyone went to church. I really didn't know people that there were people who did not go to church until I was well into adulthood. So I think I just wanted people to love the stories I loved about the Bible and the things that faith did for somebody. So then as a young adulthood it was still just a part of my life. When I went to college, I just walked to whatever church was nearest. So for maybe ten years I would go to church but I went because that is what you do. So I got upset with the preacher one year, I don't remember how old I was, but I got upset with him one Sunday because I had finally gotten tired of him talking about people from the pulpit. I walked out in the middle of the service and he was one of these preachers that always told you, 'Do not walk when I am speaking.' You know the devil just got into me (laughter)—That's all it was because I was done. So whatever it is—I was Done! So I got right up in the middle of the sermon and walked out. I decided if he asked me or says anything to me about walking out, I was just going to tell him. It was just that bad. It was Mother's Day and he had begun to talk about black boys and men and how trifling they were with their children and all that kind of stuff. I said this is not why I go to church! So it wasn't feeding my spirit with the things I went to church for. I went to church to hear love, to have and hope. I didn't go to hear somebody put other people down. So I walked out and I left that denomination. Then I went to one other church, then to my current denomination. So I think if I was to say I had a mission or goal in my adult life, it would have been for people have a faith, to be able to trust God to be with you, to learn how to treat people, just to be a good person. And that person was probably pivotal in that because it was significant for me to walk out on that. So I just wanted people to know that God was not about that.*

In my older adult life today it's about knowing God or whatever you object of faith is; knowing your object of faith, knowing what it is you believe, and why it is you believe it and living it to the best of your ability, also recognizing that God is bigger than anything or body or mistake; knowing that God is and also recognizing that mine may not be the only way. I have respect for other faith traditions and can also respect those who do not deal with organized religion. As long as they understand who, what and why it is they are this way and that they do it with integrity and respect others. You can dislike my faith tradition, but don't disrespect me in the process. If I had to say what I promote now or what my passion is now, it is that we allow others the space to believe as they believe because none of us knows. We just have to respect others and their beliefs."

Autumn—*"What I am most passionate about is self-care. Even when not practicing it, I was passionate about self-care. Holding others accountable for being well. Even in college."*

Yvette—*"Passionate about helping people even before my call. We were always helping others who did not have, even though we weren't wealthy. Felt that was the right thing to do. We always had enough to share. It intensified as I got older. When God called, I knew it wasn't pastoring, but was helping in another way and fit well with my gifts."*

Spirit—*"Initially I was most passionate about salvation. My church had very high Christology and soteriology—individual notions of salvation. It was very liberative in terms of women preachers. Not oppressive to women, so that was foreign to me. In other ways it was very evangelical and conservative. Because I was wrestling with a call to ministry, in undergrad it enabled me to develop my spiritual gifts. It was there that I realized I had a gift for teaching and administration. I led campus Bible study—it grew and I became leader. Common thread—under all the doctrine, I've always been interested in liberation—helping people to be their most authentic and free selves. It matured when I became older and developed language for it and became more passionate about it in a broader sense. So what I do now—healing and transformation is what I* do. Being full and authentic self in the context of ministry through categories of gifts that focus on helping others see their own potential and giving space for people to be who they are; and living out a prophetic call related to that. Either we're going to get up and leave the church or create the kind of church we want to be. So my church community embodies that not just in word. Reaching those who may be disenchanted or disillusioned and focusing on spirituality more than religion is important. And building esteem help while creating safe spaces for people to be authentically themselves is what I am passionate about."

Frankie—"I always had something to say about a lot of things. I was at the table or within earshot of grown women talking about things. I stayed quiet though. And they grew to depend on my knowledge about what was occurring. Making sure the message or details were correct and that justice was observed. Truth telling—I knew I had a way with words and if I used them correctly, it could affect some type of change. Been learning how to use them. In college—Challenging things that didn't feel reasonable or fair—example of being unable to take tests because of financial stress. I tried to figure out how to challenge the complexity of systems. Drawing people together to figure solutions out in the face of problems. In Adulthood—Challenging unjust systems. Was vocal and spoke truth without censorship. Had influence even as a young person. I began focusing on women as I grew into young adulthood, as a result of brief time in a particular faith tradition. I began gathering women. So continuously to date—speaking truth to power."

Jane—"I started attending church regularly at 10. Always had a special need for learning more about the Bible; Took courses, so was passionate about that. When I went to college, I had interest in majoring in religion, became interested in psychology—had passion for that and linking it to religion, was exposed to chaplaincy and really grew in passion for hospital context. Now passion is around social justice issues, reading new Jim Crow and understanding treatment of Black men and justice also the ways in which LGBT is treated in our country. So energy tends to be around justice."

Sharon—"Was very religious, came from a very religious family and in youth was very conscious of my salvation, how I conducted myself *and how I acted, what I couldn't do and was very conflicted because I couldn't do some things I really like to do—couldn't dance, couldn't go to movies. So I was unable to feel comfortable, because when I went for communion I would shake and mother would watch closely so if I didn't act joyful because I would be relegated to going to hell. Very complex and unhappy religious wise, so I stopped going to church for a while. Church fell apart, marriage dissolved—divorce—what does a young divorced woman do?*

As an ADULT—religion was modified because I start reading and took a class—Changed life. It was my starting point when you start reading and thinking about things from the judgmental God to a Grace-filled God, so began reading things differently—So my biggest desire changed to grace and love. Hate that people have to live lives in such pain and loneliness, for anyone to live like that. I am determined to fight against that. Feel that God just curls up within God's self. I am determined to be the picture of God that is a God of love—my concentration now."

Lex—"*Younger it was being saved. That your life could be different being saved. Encompassing yourself with people who were on the same track with you. I have less years in front, so I would just like to share the gospel with everyone, especially children and that you don't have to be a victim of your environment. God can still use you to do great things."*

Rachael—"*I think that as a younger person probably, generally issues of justice, leaning toward racial justice, but generally issues of injustice and fairness. And yeah that evolved to issues of race: South Africa, Anti-Apartheid, work, growing up in the civil rights era and just beyond that consciousness about race. I was conscious of race and racism early on, then gender justice and Black women/women of color. I would say as my awareness of gender issues deepened from reading and knowledge and paying attention to what I had experienced. I think I had some inklings and consciousness of that even as a younger person though—the whole boys and girls things and the way my family was socialized and the things I would object too, but I didn't have language for it. So by the time I got language for It, I became pretty intense, intense to the point I think of being annoying to some people. And now I would say that is still what I am most passionate about: African and African diasporan women, and our agency, connectivity and connection and power."*

African American Clergy Women Interview Responses

4. What are the greatest challenges you feel African-American clergy women face?

Wanda—"The barrier of ourselves. We've been taught that God does not even call us. No one should have to prove that this is so—even to yourself and your tradition. My family became supportive after they saw it was not a phase. And—All of the responsibility we have—even caring for so many others."

Violet—"That's an interesting question you ask. A couple of things—One of the things we face is being true to who we are as women preachers and pastors. We so often try to imitate men and it just doesn't work. There is a nurturing side of God and we should be able to live into that. Another thing we face is ostracism by men and women. I think that there are as many women who don't want us on the pulpit as there are men. And I'm not angry about that because I think it goes back to their socialization and what they were raised to believe. So they are living out of their own faith, but they also then are keeping people out and minimizing the opportunity to receive messages that come in a different package. When I went into the ministry I asked my mom what she thought because she was from a denomination that didn't believe in women ministers and she responded, 'God can use women just as good as God can use a man.' She was pretty forward thinking for way back then. My dad said he was fine with it the first year. Well, I don't think women should pastor, you all can preach but I don't think you should pastor. So someone in his denomination got to him and said that women are not supposed to tell men what to do. That was the difference in the pastor and preacher. A pastor tells people what to do differently than a preacher. So my father and I decided to respect each other's position on that even until today. But he would come to hear me preach. So I think a big challenge is how do we help people understand that the message can come through us? I think as women when we are in the pulpit though—in talking about the body—we have to be conscious of the message that we send with our body; because everybody in the church aren't Christian and they are not there just to get the message. And preaching is a powerful—what's the word, but there is a lot of power contained in the preacher and we add this sexual power and attractiveness of a woman—you have to be mindful of that when you are preaching and how you present yourself and how you dress. I love wearing a robe because it's easy and there are *very attractive robes, so I would say wear the attractive robe, but wear the robe. People can get distracted and women talk with their hands a lot and there is a sensual-ness with some people and their hands so you know there are still things we need to be aware of. And I think that all goes back to my upbringing of being mindful of how I presented myself as a person, as a woman, as a girl. It carries itself out today as a preacher, pastor, pastoral care giver."*

Autumn—*"Number 1 Expectation that we have to be ten times better than the best. Now remember you are the colored girl here you are not allowed the same mistakes. Number 2 Everybody really does depend on us and pulls on us and as women, symbolically we have breast and people want to suck the breast and they often suck us dry. Number 3 We don't set boundaries—we either don't know how or refuse to say no. That's a very difficult thing for us—that's a real challenge, and number 4 and if we don't fall into any of those above, then you find yourself challenge with psychological emotional, physiological issues—stress being number one. Number 5 You burn out or walk away or quit or you die; if not physically, then spiritually."*

Yvette—*"Trying to function in a male dominated situation. Even though women outnumber men in many ways, women are not taken seriously enough to do the jobs are out there. Women are the last to be considered while men don't seem to have to work as hard."*

Spirit—*"Finding genuine support is an ongoing issue. Just because women are pastoring and ordained, everything is still not ok. Sexism, patriarchy still prevalent and can impact the way even black clergy women do to one another. In and out of marriage are challenged in relationships. Courage is a challenge. Taking leaps of faith and at the end of the day, backlash will come to me. Not a lot of people can do what I do. I don't know what that stress did to me physiologically. I have a neurological condition that can be exacerbated so I have medication, I have to reach to divest myself of this kind of stress. So stress—embodied—might want to overeat, not exercise etc. Resisting fitting in and getting the acceptance of black male clergy. Not perpetuating the same stuff as a clergy woman. If you keep it suppressed you still can be destroyed by not doing what you are called to do. To thine own self be true."*

African American Clergy Women Interview Responses

Frankie—"Inability to be authentic, because we struggle with who we are which I feel is wrapped up in our notion of our bodies; what our bodies do; our relationship to or bodies; feelings of not being worthy; the notion that I can be a conduit- that I can serve as this sort of portal for the Divine to work through; and not only solely for black clergy women but many women globally. But in this particular population, African-American women have been violated and so what that does to their esteem and what ways in which they have cut off parts of themselves as methods of survival. Questions of worthiness related to being called and what that means. The other side of that is the challenge that comes with

Determining to be authentic which does not mesh with the portrayal of what a clergy woman is. It may block others from seeing me because it's outside of the box those limitations. Models are few and far between, so styles are modeled after men and even leadership is shaped by hierarchical top-down reminiscent of patriarchal values. Ways we have been taught to be subservient—just to systems. We refuse to be liberated. The propaganda—the Christian Evangelical system has really done a bang up job on us, on everybody, but particularly on those bodies that have been seen in this context of the US and really globally as marginalized and contested as not human or less than. It has done well in infiltrating our psyche to make us believe that we should be disconnected from ourselves that we should live these compartmentalized lives and that nothing good can come from this—What does it mean to tell a black person or black woman to bring your flesh under subjection? I mean what does that mean for a body that has remained under subjection since her arrival here in these United States? What does that mean to say? And what does that mean theologically to say for a group whose faith is based on this Deity incarnating this body becoming flesh? So I don't know, we just live out of 'parts' of ourselves—it almost sounds like a bi-polarity, in the sense it's a schism that is so real. If you think about it sensibly, it doesn't even make sense. It is like a ways used to police us and police our bodies, so we are just stuck trying to figure out where to be on this spectrum—can't just live in the middle because no calling would ever be fulfilled. Then of course things the usual."

Jane—"Respect. I am a part of a denomination that has only a few churches that embrace women in ministry. So it's respecting that we feel as women that we have been called into this ministry and God has *graced us to do this ministry. I am often in leadership experiences in conversation with leaders who are male trying to find my voice. There are white females in that same leadership meeting they have to work to get their voice heard. But Black women in particular who are there don't often get that same space so their voices can sometimes be silenced in different ways. So you feel you are constantly fighting to get your voice heard, to be known, and to be given that same respect as everybody else. So for me it's about respect."*

Sharon—"Voicelessness. I've felt it. You can go to a meeting. You say something and they go on to the next subject and never acknowledge your thought. Encouraging conversation and then it just goes silent. I believe it happens to us as a Black and female. I even feel that African-American males are part of that patriarchy as well."

Lex—"Not being accepted by everybody. There is disparity between men and women. Not feeling as if we have to compete with the man and focus on what God wants you to do. In society, just being accepted because you are a woman. Seeing the reality of what women really have to deal with is a challenge."

Rachael—"Being African American and being female. The greatest challenges—Apart from those two obvious ones—I think everything does stem from those two obvious ones; I think that the miscommunications, the skepticism, the distrust, of African-American clergy women, of each other, and of African-American clergy women by others. I think they are all connected to stereotypes that come from race—that are racial engendered. And I don't—it's like a really, really, really vicious cycle. So I am not sure how to be even more specific about that. So I guess I would say the greatest challenge is to live triumphantly or with purpose or as agents in spite of all those things that seem to be intersecting and challenging of the flourishing of African-American women because they are female and of African descent."

5. What models did and do you draw from to engage pastoral ministry?

   Wanda—"Those senior women and my grandmothers. I could see them as ministers in another day and time most of them would be pastors/clergy women. They were so godly, I look at their strength, integrity, just honest stuff, gentle and straight. Not a lot of education, but articulate, well- read. Some were educators. I admire the fact that I was able to compete in college because they helped to educate me and prepare me. I am still drawing on what they gave me. When I went to my first job at hospital, I stood in front of women and thanked all of them."

Violet—*"Well I didn't grow up with women as models in the church other than my Sunday school teachers [laugh]. And they wore the white training outfits, dresses and hats. So models as a pastor no. By the time I went to seminary there were a fair number of women as models and I really did have a slight problem with being a woman called into ministry myself. I think sometimes women have challenges with men thinking we are trying to take over everything.*

I had a few people serve as models for me in ministry. There were some very special women that I knew. One person told me when I accepted my call to ministry, 'Just be yourself, bring all that you are into ministry—just be you.' The other thing she told me is, 'Love the people and let them love you.' And those two things have stayed with me all these years. She was probably one of my best models. She was not one of these eloquent orators; she actually had a little bit of a stutter. She didn't try to be manly in the pulpit. She was genuine and sincere and she loved the Lord and God's people."

Autumn—*"The first model was my own mother, who is eighty-six (would have been in ministry at another time). She is very compassionate, speaks words of wisdom, is very loving and tender. Want to be more like my mother, she is very soft. The other person would be C—she had a fire when I met her that I really wanted and R has the Truth—she's the biting truth teller. And actually there are some men. My pastor A, the way he walks among people and meets them where they are. It comes from my loving—I love hard. My chaplain at college—Congregationalists pastor—A justice model I grew from in terms of changing the world. I've come into my own and they have been inspiration—I am further emboldened."*

Yvette—*"My mother and father who made room and made enough for others to be helped and fed in some ways. Painful experiences from my past and my opportunity to really see the Lord. I was bitter and needed a lot of prayer and healing. Getting through it was a model on which I draw to do ministry. Forgiveness was necessary. Were no female pastors in her church growing up. Family systems has helped me to have a model of understanding ministry."*

Spirit—"Hindsight, my great uncle—pastor of my home church, it was humility, had doctorate, very conservative on some things, but approachable, fairly large church . . . believed in strong preaching, heaven or hell, but the way he dealt with people—Encouraged people to be active in ministry if you were called. Grandmother was the pastor of junior church. Accepted call later in life. Had large group of ministers in his church and strong Bible study, reading teaching Sunday school—you did it if you were called. Saw a woman pastor and felt emotional, heard her call. Homiletical gifts. Ordained full UCC because Baptist wouldn't ordain her.

Baptist wouldn't accept her when she went to seminary with youth and children, so she worked in another denomination. Was a shared model of leadership. Wanted to embrace a model of ministry to decentralize the pastor and practice shared leadership. Empowerment model. (As a ritual practice once a month as communal practice—healing practice—use of nature to heal example of rock) health and wellness ministry as part of the ministry. ATR and various spirituality traditions. Afri-centric Christian Ministry that is holistic."

Frankie—"The women I grew up with around the table having plain conversation, the vernacular, the cues, the ways of knowing through those relationships. The everyday life experiences of Black women. Gaining and sharing knowledge from the bottom up- not a top down way. Plain talk everyday way. I need not be anyone other than myself at the table—the proverbial pulpit. Love the line from 'For Colored Girls.'"

Jane—"Two models out of my history—One was the strong black women that I grew up with. Women that learned to survive amidst great odds and who taught me that I could do anything. They never saw limitation. You can do anything you put your mind to, and if you believe that God has called you to do. My mom is that person. She created spaces for me to do it.

African American Clergy Women Interview Responses

I also had one pastor. In the time frame when I was moving into ministry, he was the one person who defied all the other men who said women couldn't preach. He was the first to bring women into our congregation, and allow them to preach from the pulpit, to say I've been waiting for you to acknowledge your call and to be ordained. So that was my model. He did not let anyone define for him what he believed about God and who God called to preach. I have been fortunate to be affirmed and supported within religious traditions."

Sharon—"Because I saw so few female ministers, I had to develop my own. I decided that I was going to be who I was. I have seen some who are dictatorial and difficult try to be like men or protect themselves from being mistreated so they put shell over themselves and I knew I didn't want to do that. So I made up mind to do things my way. Am I going to be bad, and tough and roll my neck or was I going to be myself because I'm not like that."

Lex—"My aunt being strong and holding down everything but I saw the other side of things eating her apart trying to be that strong woman. Seeing her be that, but at the same time watching her kill herself because she was not listening to her own body [tears]. She continued to encourage me, but didn't take care of her self—would still smoke. Whatever she was dealt, she managed to handle it. Also, my mom, who by most textbooks would say she was not a good mother, but I learned what to and not to do. I don't see it as shame, I see it as she did what she had to do to get by. So for now, I can identify with some of the children I minister to and use the success of my own situation. I appreciate it now and more than willing to share. ALSO—my peers and my friends, encouraging me to go forward and not stay in one place—there is something better for you. ALSO—My pastors—bishop, I see in a different light in [the] way that I should esteem a man. Taking kindness from a man and from Pastor C, harder message of take it learn from it then move from there. No victimization."

Rachael—"My mother. I did and I do because she was curious, engaging and she was accepting. She was not judgmental. She was also very open to people. She believed that everyone deserved an opportunity to live and be loved. There was a woman in my community, Victoria Delee, who was a civil rights activist and who was kind of didn't allow others to put limits *on her or tell her what to do. She was like a lawyer. In consciousness more, I think I draw on her. People who have done something and obviously has had to work to do it, is a model. Katie Canon. For the reasons that I've mentioned. You know she blazed the trails, but she persisted."*

6. How do you feel that approached has worked for you? What impact would you say that approach had or is having on your body?

   Wanda—"It's worked for me because the era I grew up in was oppressive still where grandmother had to look down, say yes mam to younger white females which took strength taught me to know that there are times to speak and not to speak, but for a different reason today. It was for survival then, but for not internalizing things today. No medication does she have to take in because she learned certain lessons about how not to internalize."

   Violet—"That approach especially worked for me—the part about bringing my full self to ministry—that affirmed that God had called me. As a person who grew up being reserved and to recognize that some good could come out of me bringing all of me into the church and that the me that I was called. I didn't have to try to be anybody else because it was Me that was called and that was good enough. And the other part of loving the people and letting the people love you—well sometimes it's really hard. For me to let people love me meant that I had to humble myself and let people sometimes take care of me which was not the easiest thing to do. It also meant that I had to let them serve me. I had no problem serving them. It was probably because I always felt I needed to be doing for other people. It was probably a way of being affirmed. And maybe it was my role because when young I was supposed to take care of my brothers and sisters, so you are supposed to take care of other folks instead of them taking care of you. The other part is that it's really hard for women to succeed in the church sometimes. I think because there were so many people who did not want me in as a pastor so to be able to love people who do not want you is really hard. I was mistreated in many ways and yet. So you have to learn how to move beyond your feelings to get to that place that is a step away that says I have to move beyond this in order to love the people. You have to realize that your calling is for them, not go back and forth with them, but love them. Love will take care of things eventually.

African American Clergy Women Interview Responses

One thing that I am aware of is that ministry lends itself to workaholism, in that we don't take good care of our bodies. And I think there was probably a part that I associated loving with doing. And that meant I had to do. I was constantly available, so wasn't taking care of my body. So my body was not the first thing that came to my mind. It was having to fulfill my call to ministry and doing church work. So I think that I haven't loved my body. I should love my body which is me—as much as I do others. If I look at what I do for others that shows my love for others, and what I do for myself that shows my love for myself, I would take extremely good care of me. I would eat all the right foods, do all the exercise and pamper myself—I haven't done that. The effect that it has had on my body has been rough. It could be that some of the stress that came from ministry and taking care of others may have contributed to my illness. I know that today I still don't take as good of care of my body as I need to and would love to. I just have discovered the joy of bed time. It came as a result of teaching Sabbath keeping. I had my students to choose children's books to read and reflect. I did it also. So I choose one that focused on bedtime. But I discovered that I looked forward to doing things for others but also need to look forward to rest and rejuvenation. So having the ways I described of doing ministry has taken a toll on my health."

Autumn—"I really have embodied them and can see a little bit of each of those people in my life. Grateful for those wonderful relationships that have helped me to make me who I am and to teach me how to love myself even when they did get it quite right. I was put on medication diuretic for a high blood pressure—I didn't want the medication but, there were stressors here at the church. So I am paying attention to any impact on my body and choosing to do what I want."

Yvette—"It has worked in that it makes me a lot more attentive and empathetic toward the people I work with. You run across all types of family dynamics. Because I have been negligent about my self-care I tend to be full speed ahead because I'm so passionate about this pastoral care thing. Started ministry for women off the street. As a result I got really involved with friendship with these folks and in the hot seat because of what they get themselves into. It holds me down because I have not been diligent for my own care.

African American Clergy Women Interview Responses

Spirit—*Has worked in terms of self-care and is still in process. Has helped me understand the importance of rest. Pray your strength and delegate to your weaknesses. My self-care has been helpful and to be in a space where people see me struggling week to week and not have to be afraid. It's ok and not shaming. My last church struggled with seeing brokenness embodied brokenness disturbed them. Has taught me self-care and importance of accountability partners. For Spiritual reasons drumming again."*

Frankie—*"The approach works wonders for me. It is liberating, it is salvific approach meaning being liberated from the fear of death. So that would be an African centered womanist method. Liberated from the fear of death either by my own hands of killing my voice because I'm trying to dim my light so that others won't feel so intimidated by the light I come with or death because I came to the world to speak truth to power. I loved her and I loved her fiercely."*

Jane—*"Strong independent self-sufficient folks. So I learned really well how to function solo and not depend on anybody, but that has also been one of my greatest limitations; because at some point in your life, you can't do it all by yourself. So the message of being this lone ranger/self-sufficient person takes its toll because you spend countless hours doing things that if you could reach out and ask others for help you wouldn't have to do it. It is also a burden for me because I tend to be a perfectionist, so spend hours trying to get things just right. After I spend those hours, I still say oh I missed that, I could have done or said this better. So I have a high expectation of myself which creates a tremendous amount of stress, which stress we all know is dangerous and harms the body. I can't turn things off, so personal life and family life can suffer so my body suffers, because you can't keep going. My pastor who ordained me literally died young in the pulpit. In word he said I need to figure out the balance, but he didn't. My models teach me how to be strong, self-sufficient, but not so much how to care for myself. They teach me how to give out, but not so much how to take in?"*

Sharon—*"It does not work that well for me. I feel voiceless. I don't feel I carry the authority I need. I'm not aggressive enough. I can't chastise in a calm and gentle way. I'm too nice and body could take a hit for that. But I don't know about it."*

African American Clergy Women Interview Responses

Lex—"Models definitely have impact on body. The message of suck it up. Also internalizing things, I see it manifest in sickness in my body. So how to handle this and knowing it can be changed. Eating right, exercising—those things can be changed. Not that models were not trying—they were working with what they had."

Rachael—"Persisting, I think it has worked well. That's how things get done. Keep going. Even if you have to stop and take a break, then come back that's just how you get things done. In terms of accomplishing tasks, I would say that works. I understand the mentor as someone who kind of walks along with you. When I entered seminary and when I entered ministry, and when and where I entered, even when I entered doctoral studies, those places and spaces were filled with men who encouraged but didn't know how to take me under their wings. There was not one who—with whom I developed a relationship or who that I can say reached out to offer a relationship. In regard to the model and my body—I think the other thing about that is that I also have my own commitments to my well-being and that I have crafted. So the persisting works for me and the way I have crafted how I live my life, so I persist and persisting for me includes taking care of myself. I think it should include a higher level of taking care of myself. Well I would say the two things work together. Because persisting—I want to live a long life and health life and I want to enjoy my older years and I have to persist in making that happen. It is part of the way I understand interacting with my body right."

7. Have you experienced negative health outcomes since adulthood—physical or mental?

Wanda—"Yes, periodically because I don't always get it right all the time. I used to get migraine. When first husband died and felt stress about raising son alone. When she lets go of things, she does better. She experienced some anxiety at one point and used prayer and meditation to calm it."

Violet—"Since I decided to go into ministry I decided to be intentional about being in therapy in some form or another either in a group or individual. So that has been a constant in my life. I have to make sure I don't hold on to this negative energy that may come our way. Plus I needed to have some way to get some of that out to make space. That's one way I have helped to take care of positive things. But yes, I do think that stress *has taken its toll on me in lots of ways. When a person is in ministry, people expect that they are always available and available to them. That meant that my sleep got disturbed from time to time or I ate the wrong food because I didn't go home and others would feed me fattening food, so it has had some negative affect on my health. And the stress too of getting emotionally involved with people that you work with and to have them die on you or to have them turn on you. And the church's hurt is one of the worst hurts you can ever have. You just don't get hurt, you get wounded. So that causes poor care of one's body and soul as well. I also don't think we take time to do the devotionals we need."*

Autumn—"Psychological and physical. The stress got to me at once why the high blood pressure came. I had trouble sleeping because I felt I needed to correct everything wrong in my life. I went through a real depression, so I decided to sit down with a counselor or two, needed to search out who fit for me. By that time, I was learning how to voice what I needed and talked with close friends. It has been incredibly difficult for me to find people to talk to because people are afraid and hold me in high esteem. I'm going to go get help if I need it. C is the person I can call to tell the most intimate details of my life. It was like giving it to God. Felt I've been healthy ever since."

Yvette—"I've learned the hard way that I don't know how to sit down (and care for myself) it's something I'm having to sit down and live with. To be quiet and seek Him more; maybe reaching up instead of out so much."

Spirit—"I had trouble standing, issues with stability, sensitivity to heat, rushed to hospital took a few years to get an actual diagnosis, ruled out many other things—invisible disability. All the mental gymnastics and having to share that in light of my vocation and public speaking.
 Learning how to live with it. Very rare condition. It's another thing in addition to being black and a clergy woman."

Frankie—"The kidney—I had only one and as a result of not knowing had complications that caused trouble, grew scar tissue as a result. Doesn't work optimally, so stabilization is the goal. Stress related factors don't help. Had a hospitalization also. Reproductively, complications with births and my body. Explored alternative medicine."

African American Clergy Women Interview Responses

Jane—"I've been pretty healthy most of my life. Took a turn in later years, not sure if it was stress related. Anxiety and depression was present, but I pushed through it in younger years. Physically, there are things that just happen related to child bearing and such. I do have a tremendous amount of stress. Blood pressure is creeping up—never had high BP. If I will keep exercising and eating right I can manage it. Surgery and hysterectomy."

Sharon—"Breast cancer, then many things, but before then I didn't have any trouble before then that I may not have noticed. I didn't have all these things that are more apparent now."

Lex—"I didn't realize when I had the stroke that it was related to ministry because I was bottling up things. Anything anyone wanted I did. She was not eating right, vitamins, exercise, all of that stuff. Had headache for two weeks pre-cursor to stroke, she was still trying to get to work. Three or four days were required for observation. Couldn't pin-point it—stress related. Just had kept on pressing way."

Rachael—"Like high cholesterol? I'm going to take care of that. I would never have thought that I would not have managed my weight better. Because I know it has to do with what I've eaten."

8. Are there rituals you engage as part of your healing practice?

Wanda—"Prayer is huge for me—embodied practice—having a mindset of prayer and try to live in a state of prayer at all times. Scripture reading, singing, beautiful music is comforting. Being anointed by someone I trust. Massage. Surrounding self with pretty beautiful things—that connects me with God and people I love. Meditation. Exercising, gratitude confessions. Stretch body and thanks."

Violet—"Sadly, that has gone by the wayside. Before I came into the ministry I studied and meditated a lot out of my own need and wanting for my own soul salvation and coming into ministry it became work. So I don't do it nearly as much as I used to so I don't get the benefit of it like I used to. But what I do now, I try it some, I do exercises at the gym. I also do mediation with Oprah and Deepak Chopra which I like. Sometimes I just have to be at the ocean. I try to go as much as possible. But that is a way that I get in touch with God, with the vastness of the ocean and the waves. And I get in touch with a lot of aspects of God, not just the good aspects of water and the nutrients it brings to the body, but also the tragedy that can come with water—because it can just change on you and you get in touch with that. Sometimes the stress just walks away just rolls right off at the ocean. Nature is a good thing for me and being able to care for myself. But I do need to do better with my rituals and devotions and meditation and things of that nature. I need to do better with that."

Autumn—"I have certain natural products I use, I cleanse my face taking care to do it, don't wear any make-up some days to give it a chance to breath. Every morning I take a bubble bath and moisturize from head to toe—it is a part of my self-care because I feel different when I take care. I also have to look at my body when I do this. Allow self to piddle. I no longer hold onto things and if I need to say something, I take time to call right then and get it out of me. Having a trusted confidant that I can share intimately with."

Yvette—[Didn't get to this question with Yvette]

Spirit—"Navigating through menopause. Some of the scar tissue how to navigate painful intercourse, who am I and what am I cut out for. Being ok with being with myself in all manner. Those mentioned above = singing bowl, Buddhist practice, learning world music. Relationship between sound and healing—no words (Spanish guy—heals brain through world music). Personal—Music, drumming, consistently taking medication, alter schedule for self-care and health. Doctor visits, water is healing—deep love for the ocean. Saying 'NO.' If something is not working for me—getting out of it more quickly. Not holding on to what is not life-giving to me. Sitting down—not pushing my body too much—figuratively and literally."

Frankie—"Alternative, energy work, rituals, foot cleansing, affirmations, body permission and healing, prayer, ancestral veneration, libation, healing touch, building esteem and reciting liberating confessions with family and children."

African American Clergy Women Interview Responses

Jane—"Seldom take medication, avoid them. Home remedies that are being regarded again today. Exercise, walk especially in nice weather, read, music quiets spirit decreases stress—whatever speaks to me, community is important, friends, family, the Bible is important to read—particular texts speak to me, listen to favorite theologian, acupuncturist, doctor annually, These are all healing practices for me."

Sharon—"No not really. Been looking for them. Devotions, prayer, but I keep looking for something that draws me. I have nothing that I come home and debrief myself. I never thought about having to do that or needing to do that. Because I always had something to do that I just want to go to bed."

Lex—"Now I take time for myself, exercise, intentional about getting hair done at shop, she massages head, still guarded about body, but I let down with her. She is very intentional—does that for me. Prayer."

Rachael—"Yes, but they are irregular. I take baths with candles. I use a lot of lavender. I spray my bed sheets with lavender. Actually that I do almost every time I change the bed. I use lavender soap. I take baths with Epsom soap and use lavender bubble bath—the lavender thing. I grow roses in my backyard—in my garden. I grow vegetables. Those I know are physically and mentally good for me. And the gardening—that is ritualistic. Yeah, the gardening—there is something too about seeing those plants grow, and working in the dirt and using your hands. It's physical exercise, but that's just healthy. It's healthy on so many levels. It's healthy because you are bending and stooping and walking around and carrying things. But also because you see seeds grow, you see the product of your work; you get vegetables you can share—yeah, there is a lot of affirmation in that. I walk in my community. I go to an aerobics class, right nearby. I do massages regularly, I have on occasion done affirmations, but that is not something I regularly practice. (When younger)—We used to use sassafras, life everlasting tea, even pine tea. Were cautioned about those who practiced using roots."

Bibliography

Akbar, Na'im. *Community of Self*. Rev. ed. Tallahassee, FL: Mind Productions, 1985.
Arie, India. "Private Party." On *Testimony. Vol. 1, Life & Relationship*. Motown, 2006, compact disc.
Ashby, Homer U. *Our Home Is Over Jordan: A Black Pastoral Theology*. St. Louis, MO: Chalice, 2003.
Barratt, Barnaby B. *The Emergence of Somatic Psychology and Bodymind Therapy*. Critical Theory and Practice in Psychology and the Human Sciences. Basingstoke: Palgrave Macmillan, 2013.
Blakeslee, Sandra, and Matthew Blakeslee. *The Body Has a Mind of Its Own: New Discoveries About How the Mind-Body Connection Helps Us Master the World*. New York: Random, 2008.
Carter G. Woodson Center for Interracial Education (CGWCIE). "The Power of Sankofa: Know History." Berea College, 2024. https://www.berea.edu/centers/carter-g-woodson-center-for-interracial-education/the-power-of-sankofa.
Clair, Michael St. *Object Relations and Self Psychology: An Introduction*. Monterey, CA: Brooks/Cole, 1986.
Creswell, John W. *Qualitative Inquiry and Research Design: Choosing Among Five Traditions*. Thousand Oaks, CA: Sage, 1998.
Damasio, Antonio R. *Self Comes to Mind: Constructing the Conscious Brain*. New York: Pantheon, 2010.
Douglas, Kelly Brown. *Sexuality and the Black Church: A Womanist Perspective*. Maryknoll, NY: Orbis, 1999.
Friedman, Edwin H. *Generation to Generation: Family Process in Church and Synagogue*. Guilford Family Therapy Series. New York: Guilford, 1985.
Graham, Elaine L., et al. *Theological Reflection: Methods*. London: SCM, 2005.
Grant, Jacquelyn. *White Women's Christ and Black Women's Jesus: Feminist Christology and Womanist Response*. American Academy of Religion Series 64. Atlanta: Scholars, 1989.
Grey, Mary C. *Introducing Feminist Images of God*. Introductions in Feminist Theology 7. Sheffield: Sheffield, 2001.

Bibliography

Hemenway, Joan E. *Inside the Circle: A Historical and Practical Inquiry Concerning Process Groups in Clinical Pastoral Education*. New York: Journal of Pastoral Care, 1992.

Hill Collins, Patricia. *Black Feminist Thought: Knowledge, Consciousness, and the Politics of Empowerment*. Perspectives on Gender 2. New York: Routledge, 1991.

hooks, bell. *Black Looks: Race and Representation*. Boston: South End, 1992.

———. *Sisters of the Yam: Black Women and Self-Recovery*. 3rd ed. New York: Routledge/Taylor & Francis Group, 2015.

———. *Talking Back: Thinking Feminist, Thinking Black*. Boston: South End, 1989.

Hopkins, Dwight N., and Anthony B. Pinn, eds. *Loving the Body: Black Religious Studies and the Erotic*. Black Religion/Womanist Thought/Social Justice. New York: Palgrave Macmillan, 2004.

Isherwood, Lisa, and Elizabeth Stuart. *Introducing Body Theology*. Introductions in Feminist Theology 2. Cleveland: Pilgrim, 2000.

Jackson, Leslie C., and Beverly Greene, eds. *Psychotherapy with African American Women: Innovations in Psychodynamic Perspectives and Practice*. New York: Guilford, 2000.

Johnson, Walter. *Soul by Soul: Life inside the Antebellum Slave Market*. Cambridge, MA: Harvard University Press, 2000.

Jones, Charisse, and Kumea Shorter-Gooden. *Shifting: The Double Lives of Black Women in America*. New York: HarperCollins, 2003.

Knowles, Malcolm S. *The Adult Learner: A Neglected Species*. Houston, TX: Gulf, 1973.

Krueger, David W. *Integrating Body Self and Psychological Self*. 2nd ed. London: Routledge, 2014.

Lartey, Emmanuel Yartekwei. *In Living Color: An Intercultural Approach to Pastoral Care and Counseling*. 2nd ed. London: Jessica Kingsley, 2003.

———. *Pastoral Theology in an Intercultural World*. Eugene, OR: Wipf & Stock, 2013.

———. *Postcolonializing God: An African Practical Theology*. London: SCM, 2013.

Leary, Joy DeGruy. *Post Traumatic Slave Syndrome: America's Legacy of Enduring Injury and Healing*. Portland, OR: Joy DeGruy, 2005.

Mitchem, Stephanie Y. *African American Folk Healing*. New York: New York University Press, 2007.

———. *Introducing Womanist Theology*. Maryknoll, NY: Orbis, 2002.

Moessner, Jeanne Stevenson, and Teresa Snorton, eds. *Women Out of Order: Risking Change and Creating Care in a Multicultural World*. Minneapolis: Fortress, 2010.

Monte, Christopher F. *Beneath the Mask: An Introduction to Theories of Personality*. 6th ed. Fort Worth, TX: Harcourt Brace College, 1999.

Moodley, Roy, and William West, eds. *Integrating Traditional Healing Practices into Counseling and Psychotherapy*. Multicultural Aspects of Counseling and Psychotherapy 22. Thousand Oaks, CA: Sage, 2005.

Morrison, Toni. *Beloved*. New York: Knopf, 1987.

Moschella, Mary Clark. *Ethnography as a Pastoral Practice: An Introduction*. Cleveland: Pilgrim, 2008.

Neuger, Christie Cozad. *Counseling Women: A Narrative, Pastoral Approach*. Minneapolis: Fortress, 2001.

Northrup, Christiane. *Women's Bodies, Women's Wisdom: Creating Physical and Emotional Health and Healing*. Rev. and updated. New York: Bantam, 2010.

Parham, Thomas A., et al. *The Psychology of Blacks: An African-Centered Perspective*. 3rd ed. Upper Saddle River, NJ: Prentice Hall, 2000.

Bibliography

Piggue, Bridget. "African American Clergy Women in Community with 'The Self': A Womanist Pastoral Theology Study Exploring Self-Literacy and Self-Relationship Utilizing Concepts from Neuroscience and Indigenous Spirituality." PhD diss., Candler School of Theology at Emory University, 2017. https://etd.library.emory.edu/concern/etds/2801ph23m?locale=en.

Ramsay, Nancy J., ed. *Pastoral Care and Counseling: Redefining the Paradigms.* Nashville: Abingdon, 2004.

Shange, Ntozake. *For Colored Girls Who Have Considered Suicide, When the Rainbow Is Enuf.* San Lorenzo, CA: Shameless Hussy, 1975.

Sheppard, Phillis Isabella. "A Dark Goodness Created in the Image of God: Womanist Notes Toward a Practical Theology of Embodiment." *Covenant Quarterly* 62 (2003) 5–28.

———. *Self, Culture, and Others in Womanist Practical Theology.* Black Religion/Womanist Thought/Social Justice. New York: Palgrave Macmillan, 2011.

Solomon, Arthur, and Michael Posluns. *Songs for the People: Teachings on the Natural Way: Poems and Essays of Arthur Solomon.* Toronto: NC, 1990.

Starmans, Christina, and Paul Bloom. "What Do You Think You Are?" *Annals of the New York Academy of Sciences* 1234 (2011) 44–47.

Stevenson, Angus, ed. "Disembodied." In *Oxford Dictionary of English*, 501. New York: Oxford University Press, 2010.

Townes, Emilie Maureen. *Breaking the Fine Rain of Death: African American Health Issues and a Womanist Ethic of Care.* New York: Continuum, 1998.

Walker, Alice. *In Search of Our Mothers' Gardens: Womanist Prose.* San Diego: Harcourt Brace Jovanovich, 1983.

Walker-Barnes, Chanequa. *Too Heavy a Yoke: Black Women and the Burden of Strength.* Eugene, OR: Cascade, 2014.

Wallace-Sanders, Kimberly, ed. *Skin Deep, Spirit Strong: The Black Female Body in American Culture.* Ann Arbor: University of Michigan, 2002.

Wane, Njoki Nathani. "African Women and Spirituality." In *Learning Toward an Ecological Consciousness: Essays on Theory and Praxis.*, edited by Edmund O' Sullivan et al., 135–50. New York: Palgrave Macmillan, 2002.

Watkins Ali, Carroll A. *Survival and Liberation: Pastoral Theology in African American Context.* St. Louis, MO: Chalice, 1999.

Weems, Renita J. *Battered Love: Marriage, Sex, and Violence in the Hebrew Prophets.* Overtures to Biblical Theology. Minneapolis: Fortress, 1995.

———. *Just a Sister Away: A Womanist Vision of Women's Relationships in the Bible.* San Diego, CA: LuraMedia, 1988.

Wimberly, Edward P. *African American Pastoral Care and Counseling: The Politics of Oppression and Empowerment.* Cleveland: Pilgrim, 2006.

———. *Recalling Our Own Stories: Spiritual Renewal for Religious Caregivers.* Jossey-Bass Religion-in-Practice Series. San Francisco: Jossey-Bass, 1997.

Winnicott, D. W. *The Maturational Processes and the Facilitating Environment: Studies in the Theory of Emotional Development.* Madison, CT: International Universities Press, 1965.

Winnicott, D. W., et al. *Home Is Where We Start from: Essays by a Psychoanalyst.* New York: Norton, 1986.

www.ingramcontent.com/pod-product-compliance
Lightning Source LLC
Chambersburg PA
CBHW022122160426
43197CB00009B/1127